A Queen's Country

To Meg and Sandy,
with good wishes.

Bob

A QUEEN'S COUNTRY

Robert Smith

JOHN DONALD

First published in 2000 by
John Donald, an imprint of
Birlinn Limited
8 Canongate Venture
5 New Street
Edinburgh
EH8 8BH

www.birlinn.co.uk

ISBN 0 85976 533 4

British Library Cataloguing-in-Publication Data
A catalogue record for this book is available from the British Library

Designed and typeset by
Pioneer Associates Ltd, Perthshire
Printed and bound by
Redwood Books, Trowbridge

To Sheila,
as always

Contents

Acknowledgements

This book was made possible by the co-operation and help of the people of Upper Deeside. They took me into their homes, dug into their memories, and gave me glimpses of the Queen's Country that I might never otherwise have known. I am grateful to all those who gave freely of their time and knowledge.

Robert Smith
Aberdeen, September 2000

Photographs in chapter 12 are reproduced by permission of The George Washington Wilson Photographic Archive, Aberdeen University Library.

List of Illustrations

1

The Castle

When Queen Victoria took up residence at Balmoral Castle in 1848 it was the countryside she fell in love with, not the castle. She thought it 'a pretty little castle', but five years later she knocked it down and built a new one. The original castle – 'a long, steep-roofed, high-gabled, small-windowed house' – started its life as a shooting lodge owned by the Earl of Fife, who leased it out to Sir Robert Gordon, brother of the Earl of Aberdeen.

It was under Sir Robert that the house became a castle, but the piecemeal way in which the new laird set about it resulted in a building with 'a jumble of styles'. With its mullioned windows, stepped gable-ends and embattlements, projecting turrets and round towers copped by 'cone-shaped roofs like magicians' hats', it was 'a very irregular edifice'. In 1850, a publication called *Black's Picturesque Tourist* said it belonged 'to no recognised order of architecture, displayed no unity of design, produced no harmony of effect, yet, when seen at a sufficient distance to be seen as a whole, might be called picturesquely grand'.

The locals certainly thought it grand. They called it 'the palace'. The people who stayed in it had different ideas. Lord Malmesbury, the Foreign Secretary, said the house was 'totally unfit for royal personages', and another Minister-in-Attendance, Lord Clarendon, referred to it as 'the scramble of rural royalty'. The house was said to be 'nearly all bedrooms', but it seemed as if sleeping accommodation was still in short supply, for one lady-in-waiting was billeted in a detached cottage and had her breakfast sent over in a wheelbarrow.

But all that was to change. Prince Albert had ambitious plans to rebuild the castle and in 1852, after the Fife Trustees had agreed to sell the freehold of the estate, the future of Balmoral was determined by a stranger called John Camden Neild – a man with a reputation as a miser. Neild, who had lived in indescribable squalor rather than spend a penny on himself, bequeathed £250,000 to the Queen. At first, Victoria thought it was a joke, but it turned out that Neild had no dependants and there was no reason to refuse it. 'I am very curious to hear what led this old gentleman to do it,' the Queen wrote to King Leopold of Belgium. It turned out that Neild, whose father had been silversmith to the Prince Regent, thought that such a legacy would give him a place in history. In a way it did, for Victoria ordered a stained-glass window to be added to his local church. She said the money would not be 'thrown away'. It wasn't; it went towards the rebuilding of Balmoral.

1.1 *Balmoral Castle*

So the Miser's Castle went up and Old Balmoral came down. The new castle was nearer the river and the view from its window was superb. Black's *Picturesque Tourist* launched into a long eulogy about its wooded haughs, 'shaggy Craig-an-Gowan', its park-like meadow, the Dee and its 'bosky' banks, and Craig-an-Darrach above 'the precipitous chasm called the Pass of Ballater'. Behind all this, it said, were 'a hundred heathery hill-tops – a "dark ocean of mountains"'.

The wilderness has retreated to a respectable distance from the castle since that was written, but a century and a half after the Queen and Prince Albert bought the castle it is still Victoria's 'dear Paradise'. Her stamp is everywhere. 'The grounds are a history book of national and domestic events within the Royal Family,' wrote Cuthbert Graham in his *Portrait of Aberdeen and Deeside*, 'for at almost every turn there are memorials.' Balmoral has become a vast museum, peppered with cairns and monuments, statues, obelisks, wells and fountains.

The first cairn was built on Craig Gowan to mark, as Victoria put it in her journal, 'our taking possession of this dear place'. It replaced a cairn already there, which was pulled down. Everyone was there, including 'all the servants and tenants, with their wives and children and old relations'. Victoria placed the first stone, then Albert, then the children, then all the ladies and gentlemen placed one, and finally everyone came forward at once, each person carrying a stone and placing it on the cairn. 'Whisky was given to all,' wrote the Queen. 'It took an hour building, and whilst it was going on a merry reel was danced on a stone opposite. Mary Symons [the shopkeeper] and Lizzie Stewart especially danced so nicely, the latter with her hair all hanging down.' Albert climbed up the cairn and placed the last stone on it – and three cheers were given. 'It was a gay, pretty and touching sight,' wrote Victoria, 'and I felt almost inclined to cry.'

The hills are studded with cairns commemorating the marriages of Victoria's children. In the Garmaddie Woods, where Queen Victoria liked to walk, there is a cairn to Victoria ('Vicky'), the Princess Royal, who married Kaiser Frederick III in 1858. Princess Alice – 'good amiable Alice', the Queen called her – married Prince Louis of Hesse-Darmstadt in 1862. Her cairn is on Creag a' Ghobhainne, the 'rocky hill of the smith', for at one time there was a blacksmith's croft below the hill. Princess Helena, who was said to be the toughest of the royal sisters, has a cairn commemorating her marriage to Prince Christian of Schleswig-Holstein in 1866, while Princess Louise's cairn commemorates her marriage in 1871 to Lord Lorne, son of the Duke of Argyll. The public, tired of hearing about Germans descending on Balmoral to marry members of the Royal Family, were delighted at the wedding. 'It was the most popular act of my reign,' said Queen Victoria. Prince Arthur's cairn lies farther north. Arthur ('Affie'), born in 1850, was a late developer and became a soldier. Queen Victoria wrote that he was 'the best child I ever saw'. He married Louise Margaret, daughter of Prince Friedrich Karl of Prussia in 1879.

Not far away is a cairn to Prince Leopold, who suffered from an untreatable disease and was Victoria's 'child of anxiety'. Born in 1853, he was made Duke of Albany in 1881 and in 1882 married Princess Helen of Waldeck-Pyrmont. Two years later he injured a knee in an accident at Cannes and within twenty-four hours the sickly prince was dead; he was only thirty-one. Princess Beatrice's cairn was built near Albert's pyramid on Creag an Lurachain; born in 1856, Beatrice was said by Queen Victoria to be 'the comfort and blessing of my declining years'. Victoria called her 'Baby' until she was grown up. Beatrice married Henry, Prince of Battenberg, in 1885 and died in 1944.

They built cairns to commemorate marriages, but death brought a range of memorials ranging from statues to drinking fountains and granite seats. A drinking fountain marked the death of Sir Thomas Biddulph, Keeper of the Privy Purse, in 1878 and there were granite seats in memory of Princess Alice, who died in 1878, and of Prince Leopold. A Celtic cross commemorated Prince Henry, who died at sea in 1896 when, against the Queen's wishes, he took part in a military expedition to end the slave trade in Ashanti.

Queen Victoria had her statues, but her memory is also kept alive by the hills and trails that she explored during her reign. There are at least two Queen's Drives: one is a popular walk running along the side of Craig Choinnich, starting at the Cromlins opposite Braemar Castle and ending on the Cairnwell road. This was Queen Victoria's favourite jaunt and at its east end it was formerly known as the Lion's Face, because of a rock which was supposed to look like a lion's head. The rock is properly called Creag a' Mhortair – the rock of the murderer – but what gory tale lies behind that I have never discovered. Victoria described in her journal how, after the cairn-building ceremony on Craig Gowan, she 'walked up part of Carrop, intending to go along the upper path, when a stag was heard to roar and we all turned into the wood'. The wood was Garmaddie Wood, where she often walked on what became known as the Queen's Drive.

Then there was the Queen's Roadie, a track built for Victoria to go by horse and gig to a viewpoint above Crathie. From it she could look down on Balmoral Castle. A number of viewpoints were given the royal tag; one was the Queen's View on the road to the Linn of Dee. It was known colloquially as the Peep o' Dee and the 'peep' you get from it is well worth seeing. From the North Deeside road, opposite Balmoral Castle, a narrow road runs up by Bush to join the old military road and in a woodland to the west of it is Parliament Knowe, where old cronies no doubt met to discuss the ills of the world. A little to the north is a big rocky hill called Creag Mhor. It is another of Victoria's viewpoints – another Queen's Hill.

1.2 *Peep o' Dee*

The Queen's journal describes how on her way to the building of the cairn at Craig Gowan she met her piper, a man called McKay, 'at the Moss House, which is half-way'. Moss houses, or fog houses, were small summer-houses built or lined with mossy turf ('fog' is the Scots word for moss), and they were all the rage in Victoria's time. Adam Watson and Elizabeth Allan, in their *Place Names of Upper Deeside*, give eleven fog-house entries, including paths and bridges attached to them, but the one at Balmoral no longer exists. 'There was', they say, 'one or more at each of the main estates from Ballater upwards, with a prepared broad, smooth path leading to it.'

There was a fog house in the Pass of Ballater near Monaltrie House, but what remains of it is hard to find. One fog house on the Watson–Allan list is the fog house of the Garbh Allt, along with the fog house path. There were fog houses near Strathgirnock, south-east of Mar Lodge, on the east side of the burn at Corriemulzie, and near Invercauld House. It is a pity they are all gone, for there were merry goings-on at some of them in Victoria's time (see chapter 2). It is interesting that the Queen had no objection to the moss house at the Garbh Allt being used by the public on certain days of the week, particularly since the lairds or their factors were opposed to such intrusion. Watson and Allan mention a 'Foggo' in their line-up – Foggo's Fence. It was a name that I heard many years ago, but in this case Foggo was a factor who tried to stop people going up Creag Choinnich at Braemar: this was on the Queen's Drive. Mr Foggo was unsuccessful. If I remember correctly, some brave souls sneaked in at night and burned down the fence.

If you had walked across the lawn of Balmoral Castle in the early years of the twentieth century you would have been faced by an awesome array of beasts and birds – an eagle blinking a beady eye at you from the rose garden, stags lolling about the grounds, dogs hiding in the bushes, and a fearsome wild boar glowering at you from the lawn. The deer were ornamental, mounted on pedestals, and the eagle sat on top of a fountain. The eagle was a gift from the King of Prussia, but was replaced by a sculpted chamois during the First World War to avoid anti-German feeling. For the same reason, Danzig Shiel was renamed the Garrawalt Shiel.

The deer were still there when the late Colin Gibson, the well-known artist and naturalist, was in his last year at Aberdeen's art college. He was asked one day if he would like to go to Balmoral and paint the deer. Colin thought they were talking about real deer and visualised himself as the new Landseer, but it was explained to him that they were life-size ornamental stags in the castle grounds and royalty wanted them painted in their natural colours. He was also asked if he would paint a sculpture of the last wild boar in Scotland.

I remember him telling me that he didn't mind colouring the cast-iron stags, but he thought the boar was a work of art and was reluctant to use colour on it. When he began he asked for a stag's head from one of the castle corridors so that he could use it as a model. It took him several days to complete them and every night a canopy of canvas was put over them to give the paint a chance to dry. Then he started on the wild boar. When he was halfway through a storm broke over Lochnagar and six gardeners came to the rescue. They laid a double line of planks over the grass and, lifting the boar on its pedestal, carried it to the *porte-cochère* at the front of the castle: there he finished the job.

I never found out what happened to the deer, or the eagle, but the old boar

1.3 *This sculpture of the last wild boar in Scotland stands on the lawn near the castle*

is still there, standing on its forelegs, glowering at passing visitors. There is a statue to a collie called Noble on the river walk and a plaque to a Chinese dog called Tchu. Noble, who was 'for more than 15 years the favourite Collie and dear and faithful companion of Queen Victoria', died in 1887. Tchu was brought from China by the Duke and Duchess of Connaught in 1890 and died the same year.

Balmoral is a storehouse of memories, some going back to Victorian times, some to more recent years. When I was researching this book I was shown a manuscript written by Mrs Alexina Archibald, Aboyne, granddaughter of George Gillespie, the Clachanturn blacksmith who made the gates at the entrance to Balmoral Castle. Mrs Archibald wrote it for her grandchildren, Emma and Colin, and called it 'The Life and Times of your Grannie'. It is a fascinating document, giving a vivid picture of life at Balmoral from the 1920s to the present day. Alexina was born in July 1923, at Jubilee Cottage, Easter

1.4 *The monument to Queen Victoria's dog Noble*

Balmoral, but her first real memory was of flitting from her birthplace to Lochnagar Cottage, with furniture in a horse and cart. She wrote:

Lochnagar Cottage was at the top of a very steep hill, and why my Father ever wanted to move to such elevation I will never know as the winters were very severe and we were snowed in very often with deep drifts filling the road from dyke to dyke.

We never had a car, only bicycles and my Father walked to work (about two and a half miles to Balmoral Castle, where he was a plumber for thirty-two years). I went to Crathie Public School at five years of age and had to walk the three miles to and from school every day – no school buses. I can remember being so cold I could hardly move – no fur-lined boots. We wore spats with buttons up the side and horrible underwear, liberty bodices and scratchy combinations.

We had no central heating, only log fires mostly – our bedrooms were perishing cold but sometimes we had a paraffin stove put in before we had the courage to go up the steep stairs to bed! Icicles hung from the roof outside most of the winter and they weren't small, some were more than three feet in length. We could see herds of deer from the house and they had very little to eat in the severe winters. We went with the lorry from Balmoral with hay and turnips and the deer followed us after waiting at the gate patiently. Many died of starvation and it was sad to see some in calf lying dead.

Alexina said that they had a very happy childhood at Lochnagar Cottage. They were never bored. They played golf from the age of twelve on the Balmoral golf course, sang in the choir in Crathie Church and at the age of fifteen were allowed to go to the ghillies' ball at Balmoral Castle. 'I danced with King George VI,' wrote Alexina. 'All members of the royal family were there, including our present Queen – these were very happy times.'

In the manuscript she tells how she visited her grandfather and grandmother at Clachanturn. Her grandfather, she said, was 'a dear old man with a great love of children'. 'Well,' she went on, 'he did father thirteen of his own, but not all survived due to TB being rife in their time. He was good to us and let us work the bellows when he was making shoes for the horses' (see chapter 6).

Alexina was born in a cottage that took its name from Queen Victoria's Diamond Jubilee, and she grew up in a royal corner of Deeside in which Victoria's imprint was everywhere: it still is today. You see it at Karim Cottage, where the notorious Munshi lived with his family (see chapter 13), at the Garden Cottage, where the Queen's Indian servant helped her with her mail, and at John Brown's statue, hidden away in the woods near the dairy. There are reminders of the Victorian era in Baile na Coille, a house built by the Queen for Brown but never used by him (his corpse lay there the night before he was buried in Crathie kirkyard); in the boat which Queen Victoria used on Loch Muick (it was said that seven kings were in it on one occasion; or, at any rate, seven monarchs – one might have been the Queen); at the Old Stables, where there is an exhibition of pony carriages and traps used by Victoria; and in the

1.5 *The house, Baile na Coile, built by the Queen for John Brown*
but never used by him

ballroom, where the ghillies drank and danced the night away – now used for
an exhibition of Victorian paintings and sculptures.

But the Queen's Country extends far beyond the gates of Balmoral Castle.
This book takes you to communities where Queen Victoria visited 'the people',
taking them gifts. It goes to the shiels which Victoria saw on her travels and it
lets you into the secret of the house with two front doors. It climbs to the
Paradise o' Pines, and tells a sad story about it. It recalls the notorious
Munshi – was he *really* as bad as he was painted? – and you can read about
John Brown and the Man with No Trousers. That and much more. Above all,
it shows you little-known aspects of Royal Deeside, not only at Balmoral but
in the 'dark ocean of mountains' that drew Victoria away from her royal
duties to explore and enjoy the freedom of the Queen's Country.

2

Royal shiels

Up in the far reaches of Glen Gelder, where the Feith an Laoigh comes tumbling down to join the Gelder Burn, a huge boulder shown on OS maps as the Prince's Stone lies half-hidden in the heather. I climbed, wet-footed, up a soggy, vanishing path to a place called Feith Ord to find it. Feith Ord was well-named – 'the bog stream of the round hills'. Wind and weather had stripped the stone of much of its lettering, but what was left told how, in October 1857, Prince Albert the Prince Consort spent a night there when out deer shooting.

The inscription was misleading. It gave the impression that the Prince had spent the night in the open air, but Albert was never a man to rough it on a bleak Deeside moor. He had two wooden bothies built at Feith Ord to accommodate his party. One was for the prince himself, the other for his servants – 'the people', Queen Victoria called them. Inside the prince's bothy was a stove and shelves had been built for 'a few boxes'. During the night it had been cold and windy, but the prince slept soundly.

Queen Victoria wrote about her visit to 'the Prince's Encampment at Feithort' in her journal. She drew a sketch of Albert's 'little housie' and thought it was 'not at all uncomfortable'. She ate her lunch at the open door of the hut, sitting on a plaid because there was no seat in the hut. She looked out over the hills and the great sprawl of Ballochbuie Forest; behind her, to the south, the moors stretched away to Lochnagar and Byron's 'wild and majestic' crags. To the east, the Gelder Burn idled past the wood where the Queen was to build a much bigger 'housie' nearly ten years later.

Queen Victoria had a passion for shiels and bothies. Whatever her love for Balmoral, it was the wilderness around it that beckoned her. The tracks that spun away into the distant hills, the countryside that reminded her of Thuringerwald (a forested, mountain area in Germany), the hilltop cairn she could see from her window, the pure mountain air – they all 'seemed to breathe freedom and peace'. It made her forget the world and its sad turmoils. She wrote in her journal that she wished she could 'travel about and see *all* the wild spots in the Highlands'. The bothies were stepping stones to that ambition, for they gave her the privacy she so badly needed. It was said that

11

2.1 *Queen Victoria's sketch of Prince Albert's 'little housie'*

when she took a walk in the castle grounds a certain protocol had to be observed. People had to pretend not to see her; in that way she could at least enjoy an illusion of privacy.

Less than a mile from the Spittal of Glenmuick, two cottages stand on an elevated piece of ground not far from the great hollow of Loch Muick. This is Alt-na-guibhsaich. It was once described as the 'key' to Lochnagar, for behind it a track from the Spittal traces its dusty way to the summit. Two hundred years ago, Alt-na-guibhsaich was a sod-covered building with one chimney, but when Queen Victoria first saw it in 1848 she made up her mind to restore it. A year later, in August 1849, she rode up the rough road to Alt-na-guibh-saich and found that 'our little housie' had been transformed.

'There are two huts,' she wrote, 'and to the one in which we live a wooden addition had been made. We have a charming little dining room, sitting room, bedroom and dressing room, all *en suite*.' The second house had a kitchen where 'the people' generally sat, a small room where the servants dined, another room which was 'a sort of store-room', and a loft in which the men slept. The only 'people' staying in the Queen's house were old John Gordon, a ghillie, and his wife, who lived there permanently.

Allt-na-guibhsaich was named 'The Hut' by Balmoral's former owner, Robert Gordon, who built it, and not, as is generally believed, by Queen Victoria. Victoria renamed it Allt-na-guibhsaich shieling, taking the name from the remains of a farm building nearby. In the years ahead, almost every lodge that she built was to become a 'shiel' or 'shieling'. She said that Allt-na-guibhsaich was 'very nicely furnished', but modestly, as a painting by the artist George M. Greig showed. Greig, who had painted interiors of the royal suite at the Palace of Holyrood, must have wondered at being brought all the way to Balmoral to paint a plain-looking cottage in the middle of nowhere. But even there the niceties had to be observed: Greig's water-colour showed Prince Albert's clothes and shoes laid out for dinner.

Those were happy days. Victoria and Albert frequently stayed at the Hut for short spells, as well as setting out from there to explore the surrounding countryside. When Albert died, the grieving Queen turned her back on the bothy. 'At Allt-na-guibhsaich,' she wrote, 'I could not have lived again now – alone.' But the Hut was to remain a satellite home for the royals; when

2.2 *Allt-na-guibhsaich, the shieling used by Queen Victoria*

King George VI fell victim to whooping cough in September 1909 he spent a month of isolation at Alt-na-guibhsaich recovering from it. Today, it is still used when Queen Elizabeth II is in residence at Balmoral.

So that was Victoria's first and best-loved bothy. The Victorian years spawned an impressive number of shiels and bothies, some built by the Queen herself, others that she passed or visited on her Great Expeditions. The image of Victoria that came down through the years – plump, heavily clothed in black, wearing a funny hat and her 'We are not amused' expression – was far removed from that of the stravaiging young Queen who rode out into the hills in the middle of the nineteenth century. She was a Munro-bagger before the first Munro Table had been drawn up by Sir Hugh Munro. Her first 'three-thousander' in Scotland was Carn a' Chlamain in Atholl, which she 'bagged' in 1844 when she was twenty-five. The fact that she did it riding on a pony made little difference. Ladies were allowed that concession; in 1801, the Hon. Mrs Murray Aust, of Kensington, rode almost to the summit of Cairngorm on the back of a pony while her four male companions did it on foot.

Carn a' Chlamain overlooked Glen Tilt. Seventeen years after Victoria's ascent of the hill she rode through the glen again on her way home from another visit to Atholl. She passed Marble Lodge, a keeper's cottage, and Forest Lodge, where she left her carriage and rode on to Bynack. It was in the ruins of Bynack Lodge that I once sat and watched a party of stalkers marching down to Atholl. The words of the 'Ballad of Glen Tilt' were birling in my head, for a hiker from Kent had pitched his tent inside the ruins and was worried that he was trespassing.

I told him of the time when the Duke of Atholl had tried to bar a party of students from going through the glen, and of how the Duke lost a famous action brought by the Scottish Rights of Way Society. I left him with a few lines from Sir Douglas Maclagan's ballad:

> For Dukes shall we
> Care a'e bawbee?
> The road's as free
> To you and me
> As to his Grace himself, man.

'We crossed the Bainoch or Bynack, quite a small stream,' wrote the Queen. She had a habit of mis-spelling Gaelic place-names, and her third attempt at Bynack came out as 'Beynoch', which she said was a shooting shiel of Lord Fife's. Victoria wasn't only careless with her spelling. As was seen at Allt-na-guibh-saich, she also misused the words 'shiel' and 'bothy'. The proper definition of 'shiel' is a roughly made hut or shed, but Victoria gave the name to solid granite lodges like Bynack and Glas-allt at Loch Muick. It was almost as if she wanted to imbue them with the kind of simple, earthy character that she saw at 'The Hut' in its early days.

There were *real* shiels at Bynack, which the queen must have seen on her way north. They were strung out along the Bynack Burn, six groups of shieling huts on the east bank of the burn, covering an area roughly between Bynack Lodge and the Geldie. The remains of these shiels, which were used during the summer pasturing, can still be seen today, as can the ruins of a magnificent shooting lodge three miles up the Geldie Burn. Here, Queen Victoria forded the Geldie (she called it the Giuly) on horseback. I had no horse to help me when I was there – I had to take off my boots and stockings and splash across the burn's freezing water to get a close look at the lodge.

Between Balmoral and the old Invercauld bridge on the north Deeside road, a little short of the fifty-fifth milestone, a private bridge – locked – crosses the River Dee, giving access to a little-known shiel in Ballochbuie Forest. On modern OS maps its name is shown as Garbh alt Shiel, but at one time it was called the Danzig Shiel, built for Queen Victoria in 1882 and named after a Danziger who operated a sawmill on the site. The Queen used three rooms in the shiel – and watched the deer come up to her window. The shiel's name was

2.3 Deer outside Danzig Shiel

changed when anti-German feelings ran high during the First World War, but even today many people still call it the Danzig Shiel.

'Drove to the Garrawalt and had tea at *Dantzig*,' wrote Victoria in October, 1890. The 'Garrawalt' was the Falls of Garbh Allt, which was no great distance from Danzig Shiel. This tumbling avalanche of water, plunging down through Ballochbuie Forest in three spectacular cascades, was often painted by Victoria, and she herself was painted there by the artist William Simpson as she worked at her easel.

The Falls of Garbh Allt drew hordes of picnickers and tourists to Ballochbuie early in the nineteenth century. The historian Joseph Robertson was raising the barriers against them long before Queen Victoria bought Balmoral. In 1832 he wrote an article in the *Aberdeen Magazine* castigating the 'pitiful nincompoops' who filled the Ballochbuie air with their 'vulgar, nonsensical chatter'. There was a kind of bothy there in those days – 'a rustic lodge' was how Robertson described it – erected by the Invercauld laird's wife. Inside was a visitors' book, signed by 'clothiers, dandy apprentices and shop boys, fresh from Aberdeen'. Some made their mark in a different way, cutting their names 'with a fifteen-penny knife on the door-post, table or window-sill'.

There were two approaches to the Garbh Allt, one by the old Invercauld bridge, the other through the Balmoral estate from Easter Balmoral. There were no 'Private Road' signs then. The South Deeside road, running west from Abergeldie Castle to the East Lodge of Balmoral Castle, continued for six miles through Balmoral and Ballochbuie Forest to the old Invercauld bridge, and from there to Braemar. Robertson noted in his article that an 'ingenious wooden bridge' over the Garbh Allt took walkers to 'an excellent road leading through this fine forest to the Brig of Invercauld'. In other words, there was a public road through the estate – and it was a right-of-way.

All that ended when Victoria and Albert bought Balmoral. Charles Greville, Clerk to the Privy Council, once expressed surprise at the lack of security at Balmoral. 'The whole guard of the sovereign and of the whole Royal Family is a single policeman who walks about the grounds to keep off impertinent intruders or improper characters,' he said. Albert, sensing that his wife's 'dear Paradise' was in danger of being invaded by impertinent intruders, used an Act of 1855 to close the section of the South Deeside road running through Balmoral and Ballochbuie. The reason given was that it was 'little used as a Thoroughfare', which conveniently brushed aside any possibility of a right-of-way claim.

After the closing of the road, the prince was given powers to provide a new bridge over the Dee, and when that was done a public notice was put up announcing that the old bridge was closed to the public. No one protested. No one cried out, as they did in the famous Glen Tilt case in 1847, that they

2.4 *The Falls of Garbh Allt*

didn't care a bawbee for a prince, let alone a duke. If that had happened, the road through Balmoral might today still be as free to the public as it is to the Royal Family. Of course, it didn't happen, and any resentment at the time was probably stifled by Queen Victoria's decision that on certain days of the week the public could still cross the old bridge to visit the Falls of Garbh Allt.

It was a promise that was largely ignored by future monarchs. Not many years ago, a sign on a gate at the south side of the old Invercauld bridge made it clear that the track beyond the bridge was not for public use. 'Impertinent intruders' were still not wanted. There is still a forlorn 'Private Road' sign on the gate, but on the north side there is a large display board giving the history of the bridge and indicating that it is now in the care of Historic Scotland. It is this sort of ambivalent attitude that confuses and irritates hill-walkers going through the royal estate.

The Brig o' Dee has been photographed and painted by hundreds of artists and tourists, as has the octagonal gatehouse near the road where a retired gamekeeper, Charlie Wright, lives. Most of the walkers and tourists who cross the old bridge come at the weekend, says Charlie. A Braemar man, he was keeper at Allt-na-guibhsaich – Queen Victoria's 'Hut' – then at Inchnabobart, near the River Muick, and he came to the Garbh Allt area in 1970, retiring in 1984. He says that deer hunting is a pale shadow of what it once was – 'There's one deer faur there was a hundred,' he told me – and he believes that the great estates on Deeside are declining. It was a view I was to hear from more than one keeper.

Queen Victoria's obsession with privacy has been passed on to some of today's royals, and the single 'bobby' looking for 'improper characters' has been replaced by an army of policemen. Nevertheless, the shutters are slowly being lifted, opening up new areas of the castle grounds and estate to the public. But as the number of people grows year by year the Royal Family's seclusion is being eroded in a way that would have shocked her Victorian forebears. The fifteen-roomed Glas-allt Shiel is no longer the jewel in the Balmoral crown; there is a detour taking walkers away from it, but with little effect, and some people walking on the other side of Loch Muick have a clear view of the lodge. Paradoxically, the track running uphill from Glas-allt to Lochnagar has been repaired by the estate, which must tempt more hill-walkers to take this route.

Queen Victoria's remotest lodge – Ruidh na Bhan Righ, the Queen's Shiel – is in Glen Gelder. 'It stands in a very wild, solitary spot,' wrote Victoria, 'looking up to Lochnagar, which towers up immediately above the house.' It contained 'only two small rooms and a little kitchen'. The Queen entertained Empress Eugenie, wife of Napoleon III, to tea there, serving up trout cooked with oatmeal by John Brown. Nowadays, royal guests at Gelder Shiel get burgers roasted on a barbecue fixed up outside the door.

For some years now the stables across from the house have been used by hill-walkers and climbers heading for the Lochnagar corries. I have often

2.5 Snow on the hills at Loch Muick. The Glas-allt Shiel is in the woodland on the far side of the loch (centre).

wondered what embarrassment there would be if a royal party turned up when the stables were occupied. I have never encountered any 'royals' at Gelder, although Prince Charles goes riding in the area, but in *Mountain Days and Bothy Nichts*, Dave Brown and Ian Mitchell described in hilarious detail what happened when a party of mountaineers, using Gelder as their base for the weekend, spotted a convoy of Land Rovers approaching. They could see 'some corgi dogs' and a 'wee loon later to be famed as Randy Andy'. They were told by a man in a trenchcoat, the royal detective, that Her Majesty wanted to have a picnic and would be happy if we left. 'We were jist gyan onywye,' said one of the hill-men, adding generously, 'Wid she like some spare soup we've left ower for her picnic?'

The outcome of this trip was said to be 'rather unexpected'. When they went back on a later occasion they found that bunks had been built in the stables, chairs and tables put in, and the floor concreted. A plaque on the wall announced that this was all due to Her Majesty. The reaction of one climber was that this 'showed she was a fine wifie, but its aa oor taxes onywaye that

2.6 *Gelder Shiel*

pyes for this and that bothy doon the road she bides in'. The Gelder bothy is now run by the Mountain Bothies' Association.

In 1993 I was asked by Her Majesty's Stationery Office in Edinburgh to write a book, *25 Walks – Deeside*, as part of a series of walking books they were publishing. One of the walks was to Glen Gelder. The book was a success, but in 1995 – a year after its publication – I was told by HMSO that Martin Leslie, the Balmoral factor, had written an eight-page letter to Geoffrey Bedford, Director of HMSO Scotland, complaining about it. He said that 'a member of the Public, concerned for the Royal Family's privacy', had drawn his attention to it. 'It never occurred to me,' he wrote, 'that Her Majesty's own Stationery Office would publish anything about the Queen's private property without first having the common courtesy of seeking Her Majesty's agreement through The Private Secretary.'

The main complaint was about the Glen Gelder walk. Leslie said that too many people were already using the Gelder route and any increase in traffic would 'further restrict The Royal Family's chance of being able to move about freely and enjoy their own property'. The fact that the Gelder route was already well known, and that the Queen had given over the Gelder stables for use by hill-walkers, seemed to be discounted. There were a number of other complaints, many of them trivial, which I answered in detail.

Letters flowed backwards and forwards between HMSO and Balmoral, there were meetings in the castle to which I was not invited, hints were dropped that the Queen was annoyed, and the need for security and privacy was endlessly debated. Thinking of the Glen Tilt botanists, my mind was rebelliously twisting the lines of Sir Douglas Maclagan's poem – 'the road's as free to you and me as to the Queen herself, man!' I was thinking, too, of the closing of the six-mile road from Easter Balmoral to the old Invercauld brig. Was history repeating itself?

I never discovered the identity of the mysterious member of the public who had been so concerned for the Royal Family's privacy, or why he, or she, had taken a year to complain. There were no other complaints. In the early days of this rumbling row I was given a firm assurance by Roger Smith, the series editor, and the HMSO executives in Edinburgh, that they would back me to the hilt, but that never happened. In the end, I reluctantly settled for a compromise. I was left with the impression that Martin Leslie had a head-in-the-sand attitude and little idea of how to cope with the growing problem of public access to Balmoral. He retired a short time later.

In 1998, agreement was reached with the new factor, Peter Ord, to hold a race through the castle grounds; Liz McColgan and other prominent runners took part. Deeside was swept by snow that day, but a large crowd turned up to watch; Prince Charles and his sons, William and Harry, watched it from the castle window. Part of the route followed the road through Glen Gelder. The race was repeated in 1999 and in the year 2000 it became the BUPA Great Caledonian Run at Balmoral Castle, with big-name competitors from all over the world.

There was an interesting postscript to the Glen Gelder row. Sir Kenneth Scott, the Queen's private secretary, had been asked for his view on the complaints. He offered some mild comments which he thought might be helpful. I particularly liked the last line of his letter. 'We have no problems with the rest of the book,' he wrote, 'which I much look forward to using myself on my next visit to Balmoral.' I wondered if the fine wifie in the bothy doon the road would also be using it.

Shiels, bothies, lodges . . . they turned up in Victoria's journal like punctuation marks. In September, 1867, one of the Queen's Great Expeditions took her to Glenfiddich, a shooting lodge belonging to the Duke of Richmond, near Dufftown. Victoria didn't give it her usual 'shieling tag', perhaps because it was too large and imposing. She described it as 'a long shooting lodge, covering a good deal of ground, but only one storey high'. Today, the lodge is in a ruinous condition and nothing has been done by the laird, Christopher Moran, a London businessman, to halt its decline.

Glenfiddich reminded Queen Victoria of Corndavon – 'Corn Davon' she called it – in Glen Gairn, a lodge once used by royal shooters. Sadly, half of it was burned down in a fire and it was finally demolished for safety reasons, while a hill-walkers' bothy across the burn was closed down a few years ago because of vandalism. Another lodge that she saw on her way to Beinn a Bhuird was in the Sluggan pass, the Fairy Glen, on the Invercauld estate – 'a very pretty little shooting-box called Sluggan Cottage, which is halfway from Invercauld to the top of Ben-ma-Bhourd'. On his way back from Beinn a Bhuird, Albert pottered about the Fairy Glen looking for stones and found some 'beautiful rock crystals'. If he had been doing it a century later he might also have found the Secret Howff. If he had done, the Queen would almost certainly have been intrigued – and amused – by what the legendary climber Tom Patey called 'the eighth wonder of the Cairngorms'.

The Secret Howff was a bothy built into the rocks above the Fairy Glen, but its exact location has been a closely guarded secret since the 1950s, when the men who built it – members of a Kincorth mountaineering club in Aberdeen – carried building material up the glen by torchlight, creeping past

2.7 *The ruins of Corndavon Lodge in Glen Cairn*

the laird's house loaded down with beams of timber, stove piping and sheets of corrugated iron. The Howff was partly subterranean, with a stove, floorboards, genuine glass windows and seating space for six. The head keeper, it was said, turned a blind eye to its occupants.

I found the Secret Howff many years ago and was given a cold reception by a group of climbers who clearly regarded it as their private property. Whether the Secret Howff is still secret is anybody's guess, but when I went back to it in 1995 it was in good condition. An entry in the Visitors' Book for 30 December–1 January 1994 showed that a group of climbers had carried up planks of wood to repair the door. They found it had already been done, so they used the wood to make a 'park bench for the west alcove'. This was commemorated in the Visitors' Book by this verse:

> Noo Jesus wis a Jiner
> And Rev. Robertson tae,
> But me and Pete biggit the seat
> Ye're sittin on the day.

The Rev. A. E. Robertson, president of the Scottish Mountaineering Council, was the first to accomplish the feat of doing all the Munros of his day.

The end of the Victorian era wasn't the end of shieling life. Members of the Royal Family still used the lodges, particularly Glas-allt Shiel. Victoria was fond of the lodge, although Loch Muick was notorious for its midges. Guests fishing on its waters were advised to wear red or yellow clothing to discourage the midges and to keep in the wind or hot sun, avoiding shady places. Paraffin oil and tobacco smoke was used to deter them and it is reported that for a time Victoria herself took up smoking to keep them off.

New shiels have taken over from the old buildings. Not far from the Invercauld bridge, tucked away in a corner of Ballochbuie Forest, there is a modern wooden 'shiel' gifted by the Norwegian government, while Inchnabobart, a former farmhouse in Glenmuick, has been converted for use as a shiel by Prince Charles. Delnadamph Lodge, formerly a croft near Corgarff, was bought by the Queen for the prince, but the house was later demolished, its stones filling a nearby lochan. Another restoration has recently taken place at the Linn of Quoich, where a derelict cottage known as Queen Victoria's Tea Room has been restored. The Queen Mother has her own shiel – a fishing bothy on the banks of the Dee near the Auld Line at Ballater.

Early in the year 2000 I went back to Glen Muick to take a look at a royal bothy I had often used in the past. There are, in fact, two of them in the glen, one at Allt-na-guibhsaich, where a building behind the two cottages has been given over to Aberdeen University students. The other is at Glas-allt Shiel,

2.8 *Aerial view of Glas-allt Shiel*

where a number of outbuildings are linked to the rear of the main building by a narrow passage. For many years a room there – the old stalker's room – was used by hill-walkers as an unofficial howff. The last time I was there it was a shambles and I wondered then if it would eventually be shut up by the estate.

The day I returned to Glas-allt was raw with the bite of winter. The road up the glen had been cleared, but the track beyond the bridge at the car park was white with snow. I had expected only a handful of cars in the car park,

2.9 *The shiel gifted by the Norwegian government near the Invercauld bridge in Ballochbuie Forest*

but it was full up, and vehicles were already lining the road. I had read a newspaper report on plans to build twenty to thirty new parking places, and there was a sketch of the proposed layout at the centre. If the car park is full up early in the morning on a cold winter's day with snow on the ground, it is hard to imagine what it will be like in future summers. Every year, more and more people head into the hills and it seems to me that the planned extension is only nibbling at the problem.

The sun shone when I set out and the hills were beautiful, but cloud drifted over and they became harsh and hostile. When I approached Glas-allt Shiel, which the Victorian writer John Mackintosh described as 'a chaste structure of two storeys', I saw with surprise that smoke was spiralling out of one of the chimneys – and it was the lum over the bothy! Inside, two walkers were warming themselves at a blazing log fire. The floor had been relaid, a wooden ladder led to sleeping accommodation in the loft (with velox windows), and the whole place had been put in order and tidied up.

What had happened? The explanation could be found on a plaque on the door. The inscription on it read: 'In Memory of Graham Leaver, who died in

2.10 *The Glas-allt Shiel at Loch Muick*

Askivalon, Rhum, in January 1988, the Glas-allt Shiel Bothy was renovated by the Dundee University Rucksack Club.' So the Glas-allt Shiel bothy looks as if it will be opening its doors to hill-walkers and climbers for a long time to come.

What the twenty-first century holds for Victoria's 'dear Paradise' nobody knows, but in the shiels and bothies scattered about the Queen's Country there will always be reminders of the time when she rode out from Balmoral on her pony in search of the peace and tranquillity that the hills can give.

3

Great expeditions

The Dubh Loch, hiding under the crags of Broad Cairn and Cairn Bannoch; the long gleam of Loch Muick, where she built her Widow's House when Prince Albert died; the forest of Ballochbuie (Frith Bhealach Ruidh, 'the deer forest of the yellow pass'), which the Queen called 'the bonniest plaid in Scotland'; and dour Lochnagar, glowering down at her through its swirling mists – these were among the places that Queen Victoria explored around old Balmoral Castle soon after taking up residence there in the autumn of 1848.

Mist closed in on her when she made her first ascent of Lochnagar only a week after arriving at Balmoral. It drifted in thick clouds over the summit. 'Alas, nothing whatever to be seen,' she wrote. 'It was cold and wet and cheerless. We set off downwards, the wind blowing a hurricane and the mist being like rain, and everything quite dark with it.' Mist or wind or rain, nothing discouraged her. On her way up Lochnagar she caught a glimpse of Beinn a' Bhuird, which was said to be one of the grandest mountains in the region. She climbed it exactly a year later.

The Queen was in thrall to the hills – to the 'seas of mountains' she saw when she climbed Morven, standing on its summit and looking out across the lands of Gairn to the peaks of Ben A'an and Bein a' Bhouird, picking out the Buck of Cabrach and Mount Keen – 'a curious conical-shaped hill' said the Queen – and nearer at hand the tablelands between Tarland and Ballater. Away to the east was the blue sea, and ships that could be seen with the naked eye. It was, she said, 'a view more magnificent than can be described'.

In September 1860, Victoria decided to realise her wish of seeing 'all the wild spots in the Highlands'. The forays into the hills from Balmoral had been short journeys: now she would arrange expeditions that would go farther afield and last several days. They would take her from the glens of Angus to the wilds of Glen Feshie, through the long arm of Glen Tilt to Atholl, over Mount Keen and down the Ladder to Glen Mark, up Glen Derry to the Cairngorms, and over the Lecht – 'this fearful hill' – to Glenlivet. They would range far and wide through the Queen's Country.

Her party travelled part of the way in open four-wheeled carriages called 'sociables' and in dog-carts (one was a double dog-cart which could carry

27

3.1 Balmoral Castle in its mountain setting, a view seldom seen by the public. In the background is snow-covered Lochnagar, which Queen Victoria climbed, riding a pony, in 1848. The mountain was shrouded in mist and the Queen said it made her 'feel cheerless'.

eight people), but deep in the hill country they rode on the backs of Highland ponies. Sometimes they covered nearly 100 miles in a day. They rode through remote villages where nobody knew them, travelling incognito, passing themselves off as a 'wedding party', giving themselves false names, staying at inns

3.2 *Lochnagar, climbed by Queen Victoria*

with cramped sleeping quarters and hardly anything to eat – 'No pudding and no *fun*,' Victoria wrote about one inn. After dinner, they sat and studied maps of the Highlands, planning future expeditions.

The Great Expeditions were described mile by mile, day by day, in Victoria's diary. Not all were classified as 'great'; some were set down merely as 'expeditions', among them an outing to Inchrory in September 1859, when they rode through country which was unknown to John Grant and John Brown. 'I was delighted to go on a *l'improviste*,' wrote Victoria, 'travelling about in these enchanting hills in this solitude with only our good Highlanders with us, who never make difficulties, but are cheerful and happy and merry and ready to walk and run and do anything.'

Four Great Expeditions were recorded in Victoria's journal. The first on Tuesday, 4 September 1860, was to Glen Feshie and Grantown. The Queen and Prince Albert left Balmoral for Bracmar at eight o'clock in the morning, accompanied by Lady Jane Churchill and General Charles Grey, with John Brown and John Grant 'on the box'. They changed horses at Braemar and went on by the Linn of Dee to the Shepherd's Shiel of Geldie, where Charlie Stewart, their guide, was waiting with four ponies, then on through Glen

3.3 *The Linn of Dee*

Feshie – 'Fishie', the Queen called it. 'We came upon a most lovely spot,' she wrote, 'the scene of all Landseer's glory – and where there is a little encampment of wooden and turf huts, built by the late Duchess of Bedford; now no longer belonging to the family, and, alas! all falling into decay.' It was called Ruigh-aiteachain.

Georgiana, Duchess of Bedford, was the daughter of Jane, Duchess of Gordon; one diarist described her as a 'bold, bad woman'. She had ten children, eight by her husband, the duke, and two by the painter Edwin Landseer. The duchess loved this wild and beautiful country – Sir Walter Scott said she had 'a passion for the heather'. She wanted to break away from social conventions and live a 'free life', and she found her dream world in Glen Feshie, 'the glen of the fairy stream'. Here, she built her encampment, a village of rough huts made of turf, with roofs of unpeeled birch. The rest of the settlement – the men's quarters – were made up of tents. Charles Matthews, an architect, who stayed there in 1833, thought it was like 'a small Indian settlement'. It was, he said, the most delightful sort of life he had ever seen or experienced. They lived rough, but never forgot the social graces. A sketch by Landseer showed the duchess receiving guests at a reception in one of the tents, with a piper playing at the entrance.

The royal party moved on, eventually coming to Loch Inch, and a mile from there crossed the Spey in a ferry: 'a very rude affair,' said Victoria, 'it was like a boat or cobble, but we could only stand on it.' A sketch by the Queen showed the VIP passengers standing precariously up in it, while the ferryman and Brown pulled at two long oars and Grant at the other end guided it with a long pole.

> A few seconds brought us over to the road, where there were two shabby vehicles, one a kind of barouche, into which Albert and I got, Lady Churchill and General Grey into the other – a break; each with a pair of small and rather miserable horses. We had gone so far 40 miles, at least 20 on horseback. We had decided to call ourselves Lord and Lady Churchill and party, Lady Churchill passing as Miss Spencer, and General Grey as Dr Grey! Brown once forgot this and called me 'Your Majesty' as I was getting into the carriage; and Grant on the box once called Albert 'Your Royal Highness,' which set us off laughing, but no one observed it.

They rode through beautiful countryside, with fine wooded hills all around the broad Spey flowing down the valley, but what delighted Victoria above all else was 'the utter solitude'. It was perfect – 'hardly a habitation! and hardly meeting a soul'. It began to grow dark and they stopped at a small halfway house to water the horses. A few people about stared at their vehicles, but had no idea that the Queen and Prince Albert were inside one of them.

> On and on we went, till at length we saw lights, and drove through a long and straggling 'toun', and turned down a small court to the door

of the inn. We went up a small staircase and were shown to our bed-room at the top of it – very small, but clean – with a large four-post bed which nearly filled the whole room. Opposite was the drawing and dining-room in one – very tidy and well-sized. The two maids had driven over by another road in the waggonette. Made ourselves clean and tidy and then sat down to our dinner. Grant and Brown were to have waited on us, but were bashful and did not. The dinner was very fair, and all very clean; soup, 'hodge-podge', mutton-broth with vegeta-bles, which I did not much relish, fowl with white sauce, good roast lamb, very good potatoes, besides one or two other dishes, which I did not taste, ending with a good tart of cranberries.

The long, straggling 'toun' was Grantown. Next morning, after enjoying 'some excellent porridge', they drove two miles to see Castle Grant, but they were not impressed. It was, said Victoria, 'a very plain-looking house, like a factory'. They stayed in the carriage, then drove back through Grantown. By this time, someone had recognised them – 'the murder was out', said the Queen. People were gathered in the street and they saw their landlady waving to them, while the maid who had served up their breakfast was waving a flag from the hotel window. It looked as if more people were pouring into the town to see them, but it turned out that they were there for a funeral.

They crossed the Spey and headed for the Bridge of Brown (Victoria spelt it 'Bruin', probably from hearing it pronounced locally as the Brig o' Broon), but stopped to water the horses at a small inn. The Queen had been worrying about the carriage horses – 'the poor wretchedly-jaded horses'. They seemed exhausted and as they approached Tomintoul the driver whipped and whistled them up the hill into the village until they looked on the point of collapse. Long after Queen Victoria's visit to Tomintoul was forgotten, the village had to live with the Queen's verdict on it. 'Tomintoul', she wrote in her journal, 'is the most tumble-down, poor-looking place I ever saw, a long street with three inns, miserable dirty-looking houses and people, and a sad look of wretchedness about it.' Grant made it worse by saying it was the dirtiest, poorest village in the whole of the Highlands.

Outside the town, they mounted their ponies and headed down the A'an to Inchrory, Brown walking at a 'fearful pace' because they were late. The sun was setting when they reached Loch Builg and a carriage and four ponies were waiting there to take them back to Balmoral. They arrived back at the castle at half-past seven. It had been, the Queen said, a never-to-be-forgotten expedition.

The Second Great Expedition took place a year later on a misty September morning in 1861, when five ghillies gathered at the old Brig o' Muick near

3.4 *This track above Loch Muick leads to Mount Keen*

Ballater with six ponies, waiting for the royal party to come rattling down the back road from Balmoral in their sociables. One of the ghillies was Charlie Stewart, who had led them through Glen Feshie. With the Queen and the Prince Consort on this outing were Princess Alice, Grand Duchess of Hesse, and Prince Louis of Hesse, along with Lady Churchill and General Grey. John Brown and John Grant were again 'on the box'.

'We rode up the peat road over the hill of Polach,' wrote Victoria. The word 'pollach' or 'pollagach' means 'full of little pools', which described the marshy land crossed by the Queen and her party. Victoria stuck grimly to her pony, but Albert and Louis had to get off and walk. The route taken on this second Great Expedition followed the Whisky Road, the old Mounth road used by whisky smugglers on the way south with their illicit casks of *usque-baugh*. Six and a half miles from the Brig o' Muick they reached Glen Tanar, where the ruins of the old Coirebhruach inn lay at the foot of Mount Keen. They had 'a very steep rough ascent' up the 3,000 ft-mountain and then descended on the other side to Glen Mark.

We descended by a very steep but winding path called The Ladder, very grand and wild. There is a small forester's lodge at the very foot of it.

We crossed the burn at the bottom, where a picturesque group of 'shearers' were seated, chiefly women, the older ones smoking. They were returning from the south to the north, whence they came. We rode up to the little cottage, and in a little room of a regular Highland cabin, with its usual 'press bed', we had luncheon.

Lord Dalhousie had come to meet them and they rode down Glen Mark, passing a well called the White Well. The well is still there, but now it is known as the Queen's Well, straddled by a massive granite memorial built by Lord Dalhousie. A small granite plaque on one of the stones is a reminder that the year of the Second Great Expedition was 'the year of her Majesty's great sorrow', for it was not long after that Prince Albert died.

They rode on to Loch Lee and the Castle of Invermark. There were carriages waiting for them at Lord Dalhousie's shooting lodge. One was the double dog-cart which could carry eight but was 'very narrow inside'. It took them to Fettercairn.

It was very small – not a creature stirring, and we got out at the quiet little inn, Ramsay Arms, quite unobserved, and went at once upstairs. Alice had a nice room, the same size as ours; then came a mere morsel of one (with a press bed), in which Albert dressed. We dined at eight, a very nice, clean, good dinner. Grant and Brown waited. They were rather nervous, but they only had to change the plates. A little girl of the house came into help – but Grant turned her round to prevent her looking at us! The landlord and landlady knew who we were, but nobody else except the coachman.

That night they all went out and walked through the village, where 'not a creature moved'. Suddenly, they heard the sound of a drum and fifes and turned back to the hotel. When they reached it they saw six men marching up and down with fifes and a drum, but nobody took any notice of them. Albert asked a maid about it. He was told it was 'just a band' and that it walked about like this twice a week. 'How odd!' said the Queen.

Next day they rode home by the Cairnie Month (Cairn o' Mount), up by the Feugh and Whitestones, changing to a carriage which the local postmaster had laid on for them near Aboyne, then on through Glen Tanar.

We drove to the end of the glen – out of the trees to Eatnoch (Etnach), on to a keeper's house – a very lonely place, where our ponies were. A wretched idiot girl was here by herself, as tall as Lady Churchill but a good deal bent, and dressed like a child, with a pinafore and short-cut hair. She sat on the ground with her hands round her knees, rocking to and fro and laughing. An old man walked up hastily and said, 'She belongs to me, she has a weakness in her mind.'

They came back the way they had gone, over the Polagach moor and down the peat road to the Brig o' Muick. Victoria said they were 'much pleased with our expedition'. They had covered forty-two miles that day, and forty the previous day – eighty-two in all.

The third Great Expedition took place less than a month after the Mount Keen outing. It was to 'Glen Fishie, Dalwhinnie and Blair Athol'. Charlie Stewart was the guide again, leading them to Geldie by the Linn of Dee and through Glen Feshie to the Duchess of Bedford's encampment. 'The huts, surrounded by magnificent fire trees, and by quantities of juniper bushes, looked lovelier than ever,' wrote Queen Victoria, 'and we gazed with sorrow at their utter ruin.' They got off their ponies and went to look at one of the huts where a fresco of stags by Landseer could be seen over a chimney-piece. They left Ruigh-aiteachain and its memories and rode on to Loch Inch, then down to Kingussie, where a 'curious chattering crowd' gathered to see them.

Next came Newtonmore – and ten more miles to Dalwhinnie, where they stayed at an inn which had hardly anything to eat, 'only tea and two miserable starved chickens, without any potatoes!' Grant and Brown were in the 'commercial room' at the foot of the stairs. 'They had only the remnants of our two starved chickens!' said the Queen, almost as if the keepers' misfortune made her own 'miserable' meal more bearable.

Next morning, they woke up to find that the local laird, Cluny Macpherson, had turned up with his piper and two ladies. A band of newly formed volunteers were on parade, drum beating and fife playing. Dalwhinnie had never had a royal visit before, and the population were out to make the best of it, even if, as the Queen remarked, there was 'scarcely any population'. It did not signify, she added sourly. The fat old landlady had put on a black satin dress, with white ribbons and orange flowers, and when the royal party left Cluny was at the door with his wife and daughters with nosegays, and the volunteers were drawn up in front of the inn.

So on they went, staying a night at Blair Castle as guests of the Duke of Atholl, then riding north through Glen Tilt on the last stage of their journey. The traveller Thomas Pennant described Glen Tilt as 'the most dangerous and most horrible I have ever travelled'. Sir James Balfour of Denmylne, Lord Lyon King of Arms to Charles I and Charles II, who drew up a list of the old passes, called the route through Glen Tilt the Potarffe pass, adding that it 'contained 18 miles of Mounth'. The correct name was Poltarffe, commonly spelt Poll Tarf, a dangerous ford on the way north. An 18-year-old visitor, Francis

Bedford, was swept away and drowned there in August 1879, which brought about the building of a bridge in 1886. The Duke of Atholl and twelve of his men accompanied the Queen through Glen Tilt, led by Sandy McAra, an old keeper, who had taken over from Charlie Stewart. Two pipers were with Sandy, playing them up the glen. 'The wild strains sounded so softly amid these noble hills,' wrote Victoria, 'and our caravan winding along – our people and the Duke's all in kilts, and the ponies, made all together a most picturesque scene.' The scene at the ford when the Queen crossed it would have made banner headlines in today's newspapers. This is how Victoria described it:

> Sandy McAra, the guide, and the two pipers went first, playing all the time. To all appearances the ford of the Tarff was not deeper than the other fords, but once in it the men were above their knees – and suddenly in the middle, where the current, from the fine, high full falls, is very strong, it was nearly up to the men's waists. We came very well through, all the others following, the men chiefly wading, and some of our people coming over double on the ponies.

So with the duke's pipers giving them 'a blaw, a blaw', they pushed on to Bynack – 'Bainoch', as the Queen wrote in her diary. When I hear the name Bynack I always think of Nell Bynack, the last of the legendary Cairngorm figures, who spent her childhood there. Her real name was Helen Macdonald, but like the rest of her family she was given the T-name 'Bynack' from the area she came from. The Gaelic for Bynack is *Am Beidhneag*, meaning 'unknown', but there was nothing unknown about Nell. She was the daughter of a gamekeeper. 'I'm hill-run,' she once told me, and that was shown in the fact that she acted as unofficial guide to many hotel guests from Braemar. She had been to the top of Ben Macdhui twenty-two times.

The Queen's spelling of Bynack as Bainoch is understandable, for, as often happened, there were a number of alternatives, among them the Burn of Baynock. The Duke of Atholl took his leave of the queen at Bynack Lodge, whose ruins still lie there today. The duke gave the Queen some whisky out of an old silver flask and proposed her toast, then he and his men turned and went back down the Tilt in the dark while Victoria pushed north on the last lap to Balmoral. 'We had travelled sixty miles today,' she wrote in her journal, 'and sixty yesterday. This was the pleasantest and most enjoyable expedition I *ever* made.'

A week later the Queen and Prince Albert were off again to the hills above the Cairnwell. With them were Princess Alice, Prince Louis and Lenchen, who was Princess Helena, the Queen's fifth child. Victoria said she had 'great difficulties with her figure', but she was practical and businesslike and believed in speaking her mind. It was a cold, crisp morning, with frost on the ground and a bright blue sky when they set off for the Cairnwell. The Queen thought that the mountains had a shade of blue 'like the bloom on a plum'. It was a much shorter journey this time, without an overnight stay, and it took them across a vast tableland where the hills seemed to stretch away to the edge of the world.

They were treading an ancient pass from Braemar to Glen Isla. The Queen, who could never remember names, called it Month Eigie, which was probably as near as she could get to the Gaelic – *mon-eagach*, a mount with notches on it. It was better known as the Monega Pass. It was a right-of-way Mounth pass – the highest public path in the country – and the original approach to it was by the Seann Spittal (Old Spittal) bridge, near the Cairnwell road. As the name suggests, there was a hospice there at one time. From there the route lay across the Cairnwell Burn, up the steep, rough face of Sron na Gaoithe and round the eastern shoulder of the hill. Today, hill-walkers make a more direct approach to it from the ski centre to Glas Maol. The royal party returned by Sron na Gaoithe, but began their climb at Loch Callater, where their ponies were waiting. The ponies took them up to Carn an Tuirc, the hill of the boar.

'Going up Cairn Turc,' wrote Victoria, 'we looked down upon Loch Canter, a small loch above Loch Callater, very wild and dark.' One poet wrote about it as 'lonely, lonely dark Loch Kander'. High on the corrie above the loch are the ruins of an old shepherd's bothy, which the Queen may have seen. There is nothing in her diary to show that she did, but the bothy was in use when she passed that way. Professor William McGillivray, the naturalist, saw it in 1850, and noted that there was a place in the bothy for a small fire, two stone benches and two recesses in the wall for pipes and other articles. One of the benches can still be seen and there is still a hole in the wall for the shepherd's pipe.

Riding over the tableland on her pony, Fyvie, Victoria marvelled at 'the wonderful panorama which lay stretched out before us', taking note of the mountains she could see: Bein Macdhui, Braeriach, Ban Avon, Bein a' Bhuird, then Bein a'Ghlo and Shiehallion, west to Ben Nevis, and south to the Lomond hills.

> Another half-hour's riding brought us to Cairn Lochan, which is indeed a bonnie place . . . a narrow valley, the river Isla winding through it like a silver ribbon, with trees at the bottom. The hills are green and steep, but towards the head of the valley there are fine precipices. We sat on a very precipitous place, which made us dread anyone's moving backwards, and here we lunched.

Up on the Caenlochan plateau it was bitterly cold. On top of Carn an Tuirc they found 'ice thicker than a shilling'. Prince Albert wrote on a bit of paper that they had lunched there, then put it into a bottle and buried it there, 'or rather stuck it in the ground'. John Grant had apparently done the same thing when they climbed Bein Macdhui, so these royal messages may still lie up on that frozen tableland.

The keeper Duncan wrote out an account of their route because the Queen could never 'mind' the names. Her head, she said, was 'so very ungeographical'. They came down by Cairn of Claise and Garbh-choire, following the 'Month Eigie Road'. Down 'a steep hill covered with grass, part of which I rode, walking where it was steepest, but it was so wet and slippery that I had two falls'.

They reached the Spittal bridge and then 'down along the new road, at least that part of it which is finished, and which is to extend to the Cairn Wall'. She could never have imagined that a century later that 'new road' would be carrying thousands of skiers up the Cairnwell, that the hills she had admired would be ugly with ski-lifts, and that the old Monega Pass would be left to passing hill-walkers. 'The moon rose and shone most beautifully,' she wrote, 'and we returned much pleased and interested with this delightful expedition.

3.5 *Deer at the Spittal of Glen Muick*

Alas! I fear our *last* great one!' Two months later Albert was dead, and when her journal was published in 1870 the Queen had a footnote to the Monega diary: '(It was our last one! – 1867)'.

4

Land of rashes

Heavy clouds hung over Lochnagar on the day that I climbed up through the vast forestlands of Birkhall to the Coyles of Muick. The wind snapped and snarled round a crumbling cairn on one of the tops and the first spits of rain came blustering down the glen. I had gone to the Coyles to get a birds-eye view of Birkhall, half hoping it would be an eagle's eye view. I was a century too late.

'Eagles are at times yet seen on the Coyles,' wrote the Deeside historian Alex Inkson McConnochie. 'No less than six were seen on a certain occasion "hunting" a wounded stag.' That was in 1891 when these kings of the air were a familiar sight on Upper Deeside. There is a cliff above the Dubh Loch whose highest point is called Creag na h-Illaire, the Eagle's Rock. Eagles had their eyries there, but they eventually abandoned it. McConnochie also told of a pair of young eagles breeding on a tree near Abergeldie Castle. Two of the young birds were taken to Balmoral Castle, but nothing is said about how long they stayed there or what happened to them.

The first time I climbed the Coyles I lost my way in a maze of tracks that dissects Alltcaillich Forest, wandering about until I came to a wooden hut – Queen Victoria would have called it a bothy – built for Prince Charles. There was no furniture in it, only a broom to sweep away the picnic crumbs, but I ate my sandwiches on a heathery bank outside. The Queen Mother often walked with her dogs in this sprawling woodland, meeting and chatting with passing hill-walkers. The forest, incidentally, takes its name from a stream called Allt-na-Caillich, 'the old wife's burn'.

My stravaiging also took me to the Craig of Loinmuie, another of the Coyle's tops. It looks down on the vanished clachan of Loinmuie, which I wrote about in *Land of the Lost*.

The Coyles consist of serpentine rock, which runs north for nearly two miles in what McConnochie called 'several bare peaks', but it has never been made clear how many peaks are regarded as Coyles. McConnochie plumped for three, but gave the highest top as *the* Coyle. The others were Craig of Loinmuie and Creag Bheag. On the other hand, that classic book *The Cairngorms* ignored Creag Bheag and identified the third Coyle as Meall

Dubh, a dark, lumpy hill whose only claim to fame was that it once had a slate quarry which provided black slates for Birkhall House.

The Ordnance Survey map of 1869 shows all the four tops, but only one is given the name 'Coyle'. So there is little doubt that there was originally only one real Coyle of Muick – the rest must bask in its reflected glory.

In tiny print beside the name Creag Bheag are the words 'Prince of Wales's Cairn'. In 1863, Queen Victoria chose Creag Bheag as the peak on which to build a cairn commemorating the marriage of the Prince of Wales (later Edward VII) to Alexandra, Princess of Denmark: the weather made short work of it. The cairn became so ruinous that Victoria decided to build another one on a higher top – the main Coyle. Again the weather won, for by the turn of the twentieth century McConnochie was writing, 'The elements have not paid much respect to this cairn.' He might have been writing about today, for when I was there half the cairn had fallen into the heather. The stone plaque on it had disappeared and I found it lying in the heather well down the hill;

4.1 *This stone plaque commemorating the marriage of the Prince of Wales (later Edward VII) to Princess Alexandra of Denmark was formerly on the cairn on the Coyles of Muick; now it is halfway down the hill*

the inscription read: 'Erected by Command of Queen Victoria.' She would not have been amused.

I left the Coyles in dripping rain and made for a farm which sounded as if it might have resigned itself to such *dreich* weather. Dorsincilly stands on the banks of the Muick between Birkhall and the Brig o' Muick. The name has a romantic ring about it, but the reality is different. The place-name experts bring you down to earth with a splash. Adam Watson and Elizabeth Allan in their *Place-Names of Upper Deeside* gave the meaning as 'the passageway of the shedding or dripping, i.e. a wet place'. William M. Alexander's *Place-Names of Aberdeenshire* said it was 'the passageway of the *silleadh* – a dripping, oozing place'. The word 'passageway' is puzzling. Another place-name expert, James Macdonald, said that the name was obscure, but might 'refer to some old cross-roads not now existing'. Dorsincilly looks across the Water of Muick to Balintober, where the ruins of old settlements are scattered along the glen, and an old Whisky Road climbs away to Cairn Leuchan and crosses the moors to Glen Tanar. There was a ford at Dorsincilly at one time and later a foot-bridge and it may be that they were links in the 'passageway' that led to the whisky trail, well away from gaugers on the look-out at the Brig o' Muick.

Down in Dorsincilly I met Mike Anderson, the farmer. With him was Joan Elrick, who had worked with me in my newspaper days. 'What about this wet place?' I asked. Mike laughed. 'Some folk have another name for it,' he said. 'They call it Land of the Rashes.' Mike was born at Dorsincilly. He knew about the ford, but had never heard of a bridge. He took me across the fields to where the ford was hidden in a loop of the river not far from the Brig o' Muick. It was a tranquil corner, which he knew well. He swam there when he was a lad and fished with a pal for trout: 'wee trout!' he said. The gamekeeper turned a blind eye on the young poachers.

On the other side of the ford was the house where the Deeside artist Howard Butterworth lived and beyond it Birch Cottage, the home of journalist Ken Adams, whose father, Norman Adams, writes books about crime and ghosts. I wondered if he knew that there was a ghost – the Green Lady – at Birkhall House or that a miller at Milton of Braichly had claimed to have seen fairies in the mill.

I wouldn't have been surprised if there had been ghosts on Knock Hill, for it carries the grisly memory of the seven sons of Alexander Gordon of Knock, who were slaughtered by Alexander Forbes of Strathgirnock. He cut off their heads, stuck them on the cross-tops of the flaughter spades (peat-cutting spades) they were using and lined up these gory trophies on the hillside. When the laird of Knock heard the news he fell down the stairway of the castle and was killed. Forbes was hanged in his own house for the crime and Knock, along with Birkhall, went to Gordon of Abergeldie.

4.2 *Mike Anderson, the farmer at Dorsincilly, is seen at the old ford on the River Muick*

I never heard any tales of ghosts on Knock, and if there had been Mike would probably have heard about them, for he farms the land on which the old castle stands. In recent years he has taken over the farmlands of Knock, Alltcaillich and Toldhu. He has seen change come blowing down the glen, sweeping away old traditions, wiping out a way of life that set the Land of Rashes apart from other communities. Mike could remember how as a boy he had watched a string of forestry workers on bikes coming up the glen every morning. When he went to school at Ballater all the pupils from Birkhall were taken there in a big Strachan's bus. Later it was replaced by a smaller bus, then there was a mini-bus, and finally a car: now even the car has gone. The local hall stands empty and unused, but at one time the WI met in it and there were whist drives and Christmas parties there. All that has gone. The cottages in the area are either holiday homes or they house the Balmoral staff and guests when the present queen is on Deeside.

The Dorsincilly brig was one of a number of footbridges spanning the Muick, lifelines between the communities on either side of the water, opening up 'passageways' to the south by the Capel Mounth. In *The Place-Names of Upper Deeside* the names of these bridges were given as they were spoken. A foot was a 'fit', so a footbridge was a fitbridge – the Aucholzie Fut Brig, for instance, and the Birkhall Fit Briggie, not far from the Birkhall Haughie. The whole length of the Muick was measured by fords and footbridges that kept the traffic flowing; men, cattle, ponies and eventually carts. The first wheeled cart used at Inchnabobart was brought to Deeside early in the nineteenth century. Four men with two horses took it over the Capel from Kirriemuir.

At Inchnabobart a stream called Allt a' Mhaide, 'the fox's burn', joins the Muick and is crossed by a small stone bridge. The street was originally known as 'the burn of the two sticks' because it had a bridge made from two trees laid lengthwise across the water. The Fox's Burn was close to what was one of the most important crossings of the Muick – the Inchnabobart ford. Drovers going to markets in the south pushed great herds of cattle across the Muick and halted for the night at the inn at Teetaboutie, whose ruins can still be seen on the road to the Spittal of Muick. There, too, Queen Victoria forded the Muick on her way to Loch Muick or when setting out on her Great Expeditions.

4.3 *Inchnabobart Ford*

'We drove beyond Inch Bobard,' she wrote in her journal, 'changing horses near Birkhall and stopping for a moment at the Linn of Muich.'

The Inchnabobart ford existed before there was a road on the left (west) bank of the Muick. When the road was made a footbridge was built, but it was taken down in 1863. A. I. McConnochie argued that it should be replaced. He thought it would 'be a great convenience to the public', for they could then cross the river at Inchnabobart instead of tramping up to the Spittal and coming back by the road on the west side of the Muick.

Why the Inchnabobart bridge was demolished and never rebuilt no one knows, but it is more than likely that Queen Victoria wanted to discourage the public from using this 'back door' into the royal estate. There was at one time a ruinous wooden bridge across the Muick at Allt an t-Sneachda, the snowy burn, where traffic crosses a cattle grid as the woodland gives way to open moor on the run-up to the Spittal. I remember how, year by year, the old bridge rotted away until finally it was gone. The feeling was that Balmoral had quietly cut off another access to the Inchnabobart road. There were rumours that the Duke of Edinburgh was behind the removal of the bridge.

Until 1836 the driving road on the right bank of the Muick, now the main route up the glen, came to a halt at the Inchnabobart ford. The farm at Inchnabobart has the highest cultivated land in the glen, but the farmhouse has now become another Balmoral howff. The name Inchnabobart is said to mean 'the field of the poet's cow'. James Macdonald dismissed this romantic theory as 'worthless', putting forward the alternative 'the meadow of the cow's dyke'.

It used to be said on Donside that people going to Bennachie had to go down the Lord's Throat, but on Deeside you have to go down the Cock's Neck to get to Birkhall. About a mile from the Brig o' Muick a side road slips away from the main glen road and crosses the Muick to the Mill of Sterin. It is a mad little road, swooping steeply down to the river and twisting and turning through a series of sharp bends like a miniature version of the old Devil's Elbow. Local folk thought that this short stretch of road looked like a cock's neck – and that's what they called it.

The Cock's Neck road links up with the road to Inchnabobart, where there is a notice telling you that it is private. McConnochie said that the road on the Balmoral side above Inchnabobart was 'held by some to be public'. The record in the National Catalogue of Rights of Way notes that there was vehicular use of the road until at least 1939. This could mean that the reduced use of vehicles during and after the war brought about the lapsing of the right of way. It is still, however, regarded as at least a pedestrian right of way. In recent years the Balmoral estate has been undertaking a review of all access on the estate.

There was a ford with stepping stones at the bottom of the Cock's Neck. I

4.4 *The Cock's Neck, the twisting road down to the mill of Sterin*

entered Birkhall by this route because I was intrigued by the name Sterin. Birkhall was originally called Sterin, which comes from *stairean*, meaning 'stepping stones'. Today, the name is retained only in the old mill; McConnochie called it a 'clattering mill', but this may have had more to do with stones than noise. William Alexander said that the word 'clattering' was often used to describe wet places crossed by stepping stones.

The mill of Sterin was formerly a meal mill, but after 1838 when the glen began to feel the bite of depopulation meal mills became redundant and Sterin became a sawmill. There was also a cornmill at Aucholzie. When I was at Sterin there were two 'pony' girls from Balmoral living in the mill house. The mill itself is a forlorn building, but at one time it was used as a social centre and a ballroom. Opposite it is a vacant piece of ground where one of Balmoral's 'bobbies' had a cottage. His legacy to tourists tearing down the Cock's Neck is a garden which has been swamped by wildflowers, bringing a splash of colour to the 'clattering mill'. Beside the bridge over the Muick is a keeper's house which was once the school. During the Second World War, Marion Crawford – 'Crawfie', the royal children's governess – organised weekly sewing parties in the schoolroom. The school closed in 1949.

In a field flanking the road from the Brig o' Muick to Knock Hill a standing stone can be seen in splendid isolation. Some people say it is a scratching stone for cattle, but, in fact, it is much more than that. It is shown on some maps as the Scurriestone, or Scurry Stane. There are different theories on the origin of the name. One is that it comes from the Gaelic *Sgarbhaidh*, 'a crossing of the river by a ford', and, significantly, the field in which it stands was once known as *Roinn a' Chroisg*, the 'land portion of the crossing'. According to Macdonald, there was an old ford on the Dee not far from the stone. 'This stone', wrote Macdonald, 'may have marked the spot where the road branched to the fords of Dee and Muick'.

So we are back in the world of fords and crossings, those vital links in the life of Upper Deeside. Yet the 'monument' theory has some appeal, for in a sense the Scurriestane *is* a monument – a signpost to a long-forgotten past.

4.5 *The mill at Sterin*

Across the road is the farm of Dalliefour, which Adam Watson and Betty Allan said was 'often called Scurriestone locally'. This isn't surprising, for at the end of the nineteenth century the farm was known as Scurry Stone Farm, and there was also a Scurry Stane Chapel. All traces of the chapel have gone.

There was another church near here, the old parish church at the Brig o' Muick. In the kirkyard at the Brig the bones of John Mitchell lie under a coffin-shaped slab with the lettering '1596 I.M. 1722'. Mitchell, a well-known poacher, lived to the age of 126. His home was at Dalliefour. The church at the Brig wasn't much of a kirk, for in the year that Mitchell died the Statistical Account described it as 'a very old house thatched with heath'.

In 1798 a new church was built in Ballater on the site of the present parish church. On the night the foundation stones of the new church were laid the old thackit kirk was burned down. The blame was laid at the door of the minister's wife – and her hens' eggs. It was said that she kept hens' nests inside the kirk and the maid, looking for eggs with a lighted bit of fir, set fire to the building.

4.6 *The old school at Sterin, now a private house*

The road to Birkhall cuts away from the South Deeside road at the foot of Knock Hill, leaving the ancient tower with its gory memories. A. I. McConnochie thought that the Abergeldie lands should be part of the royal estate because they were adjacent to Balmoral. 'The two would make a very compact property,' he wrote, 'especially when it is considered that Birkhall, also belonging to the Queen, lies next to Abergeldie on the east and near to Balmoral forest at its south-east boundary.'

When the Prince Consort bought Balmoral for £31,500 in 1852 he also had his eye on Birkhall, Ballochbuie Forest and Abergeldie. Albert bought Birkhall for the Prince of Wales in 1862, but in 1885 Edward sold it to his mother and it became part of the Balmoral estate. Ballochbuie was also bought, but the Gordons resisted all attempts at a royal takeover of Abergeldie. Instead, they leased it to the Queen. With this lease, the royal estates covered 40,000 acres, stretching along the right bank of the Dee for half-a-dozen miles and sweeping back to Lochnagar. It included two great deer forests – Balmoral and Ballochbuie – holding a stock of about 800 stags and 500 hinds.

Birkhall House was built early in the eighteenth century by Charles Gordon and his wife, Rachel, who was the tenth laird of Abergeldie. The Statistical Account for 1791–99 described 'Mr Gordon's farm of Birkhall' as an example of what could be done with the land. He built stone fences and hedges, levelled and straightened the fields, drained marshes, and raised 'bear, oats, pease, potatoes, turnips and hay of as good quality as any in Aberdeenshire'. He also paid attention to neatness and elegance, 'clearing away the rubbish of nature and displaying her beauties'.

This was a Jacobite home, built in 1715, the year of the first Jacobite Rising, and in 1746 it gave shelter to two people fleeing from Culloden – the Oliphants of Gask. They moved about the country under the adopted names of Mr Brown and Mr White and sent their belongings to friends for safekeeping. Most of it was 'delivered to Mrs Gordon at Birkhall', including 'a sute of Hyland Cloaths and Phylibeg'. There was also a pair of 'red ever-lasting britches'. The Oliphants eventually escaped to Sweden and Mrs Gordon wrote to Lady Gask to say, 'Mr White and Mr Brown is in good health'.

Mr White and Mr Brown were the first in a long line of prominent people who stayed at Birkhall over the years, particularly during Queen Victoria's reign. Among them was the Duchess of Albany – Princess Helen of Waldeck and Prymont – who married Queen Victoria's youngest son, Prince Leopold. He died suddenly in 1884 at the age of thirty-one. The Queen's doctor, Sir James Clark, also lived there for a number of years, and it was during his residence, in 1856, that Florence Nightingale visited Birkhall as the guest of the Queen. It was there that she persuaded Lord Panmure, the Secretary of State for War, to set up the Royal Army Medical Corps.

Florence Nightingale's sister, Parthenope, was a guest of Sir James Clark and Lady Clark when they were on a family holiday at Birkhall. Florence Nightingale, as her name suggests, had been born in Florence, and her sister Parthenope was born in Naples and named after a siren in Greek mythology, who drowned herself when Odysseus evaded the lure of the sirens' singing, her body supposedly cast ashore at what became Naples. Parthenope Nightingale was said to be a highly neurotic woman.

Sir James Clark, whose diagnosis was often said to be suspect, became involved in what was known as the Lady Flora scandal. Lady Flora Hastings, the Duchess of Kent's lady-in-waiting, was a spinster in her early thirties with a sharp, malicious wit. Queen Victoria detested her, referring to her as 'that odious Lady Flora'. Over Christmas 1838 Lady Flora suffered from violent pains in the stomach; too much turkey and plum pudding, they said, but the pains persisted. She consulted Sir James several times, but he never once examined her undressed. Tongues wagged and rumours spread; Sir James said he was sure that Lady Flora was pregnant, but he advised that the wisest thing to do was to wait and see. She died in the summer of 1839, a post-mortem showing the cause of death to be a tumour of the liver.

Birkhall has cast its spell over a long line of kings and queens, princes and princesses, lords and lairds. The birch haugh is in part of the Queen's Country that is gradually being opened up to the public, yet it has remained isolated from tourists and hillwalkers. Princess Alice, Countess of Athlone, recalled in her memoirs how her family had spent some of the happiest days of their lives there. 'It was a small place in those days,' she wrote. 'We loved the sloping garden full of fruit and sweet peas and, at the bottom, a chain bridge, heavenly to jump upon, which spanned the rushing little Muich where we loved to play. As there were only horse-drawn vehicles, Birkhall was one of the stopping places for the deer stalkers to drop in for a vast tea of scones and cakes and jam.'

It came into its own again as a family home during the reign of King George V, when the Duke and Duchess of York and their daughters, Princess Elizabeth and Princess Margaret, made use of it. In 1936, when the duke became king, Balmoral became their official Scottish home and there were no more visits to Birkhall until war broke out. In 1939, evacuees from Glasgow were sent to Deeside – and Princess Elizabeth and Princess Margaret came north to Birkhall as royal 'evacuees'. Their governess, Marion Crawford, wrote about it in her book *The Little Princesses*. 'The King opened up Craigowan, a large house on the Balmoral estate, for evacuees, where they lived in positively ducal surroundings. Alas, very few appreciated it. The children were terrified of the silence, scared to go into the woods, and frightened if they saw a deer. Some there were who wanted to take the next bus back to Glasgow. "Oh, the awful quiet!" they said.'

After the war Princess Elizabeth took over Birkhall and when she married Prince Philip in 1947 part of their honeymoon was spent there. 'It was up at the quiet little house Birkhall that their real honeymoon began,' wrote Crawfie. 'Birkhall had so many happy memories. The wide moors took them to their hearts. The country folk, with traditional Scottish courtesy, left them alone.' Crawfie's book ended with her remembering Birkhall, and the moors behind, wine red, the air full of the scent of wood smoke, and coming over the grass towards her three figures, all dressed in blue – 'the little Duchess and her two daughters, as I knew them first, long ago'. Sadly, *The Little Princesses* ended Marion Crawford's relationship with the Royal Family. Although it was written after she had left them, the fact that she had written it at all was regarded as a breach of protocol. All contact with her ended – Crawfie was sent to Coventry.

When King George VI died in 1952, there was a change of Deeside homes, the new Queen moving to Balmoral, and Queen Elizabeth, the Queen Mother, making Birkhall her Scottish home; she was then able to bring to fruition the plans she had had for Birkhall while staying there as Duchess of York. A new wing was built for guests and the garden was laid out with alpine plants and roses. Half a century later, in the year 2000, people were hoping that the Queen Mum would come back to Birkhall to celebrate her 100th birthday.

5

Paradise o' pines

It was a land where eagles flew, beating the sky above the 'cleughs o' Bachnagairn' as they soared 'owre heather bells and fern', and in the morning the sun came up with its 'rosy neb a' tipped wi' gowd'. It was an idyllic place, even at the back end of the year when winter put its cold hand on the hills and 'busked their heads wi' snaw'. It inspired one poet to write about the yellow, winding pathway that led to 'the Paradise o' Pines at Bachnagairn'.

The Angus poet, Dame Maria Ogilvy of Clova, dipped into a heady brew of Doric to write about Bachnagairn. The lines of her poem were often in my mind when I climbed up to it by 'bauld Braid Cairn', feeling the winds blowing off the Capel Mounth, or when I tramped through the broad Clova valley, up under the dark brows of Juanjorge and the slopes of Dog Hillock, where an avalanche once killed nearly forty deer. When I passed the keeper's house at Moulzie I saw a fox's skin pinned to a door. It reminded me of another poem that the painter Edwin Landseer wrote in a game-book in Glenfeshie:

> The boards so green were hung around with
>   The skins of cats and foxes
> All sat by day on wooden chairs and slept
>   in wooden boxes.

Bachnagairn is a long strip of woodland draping the banks of the South Esk as it tumbles down from Loch Esk near the old county boundary. About a mile below the loch the river drops through a deep ravine, plunging down about seventy to eighty feet, and from there it cascades away to the glen below, bouncing over rocks worn smooth and flat by the endless torrent of water. A number of years ago there was a wooden bridge over the ravine, a dilapidated structure that always looked as if it would disintegrate when you were halfway over.

I came to know about it some fifteen years ago when I was standing on the path above Bachnagairn, looking down on the trough of the Esk. Some distance away I could see a tractor and bogie at the edge of the track, unable to overcome that last steep climb to the bridge. I could hear the whine of an

5.1 *The old bridge at Bachnagairn, with the waters of the River Esk tumbling some 70 ft down into the ravine below*

electric saw and see tiny figures moving among the fallen timber. They were building a new Bachnagairn bridge – and how it came about is a story to touch the heart.

It was up that path from Moulzie that a climber called Roy Tait often came, his hill-boots clumping over the old bridge as he crossed it from Angus to Deeside and went on to the corries of Lochnagar. He belonged to Aberdeen, but lived and worked in Dundee. He had a soft spot for Bachnagairn, as had his wife Shirley, for here the hard, unyielding face of the hills can soften to a beauty seldom seen in such places. He was never away from the hills, but one day he made his last journey to Lochnagar: he was killed in an accident in one of its corries.

Roy would have appreciated Dame Maria Ogilvy's poem, with its tongue-twisting lines about the 'yammering yearn' (eagles) and 'the prood gorcock [red grouse] chittering on the Sneck o' Barnes'. He himself was a poet of sorts, his verse mocking at the dangers faced by climbers, at the hill-man who laid six to four that his luck wouldn't run out, at people who did their best climbing in the pub, and at the cautious hill-man whose footwork was perfect – two feet from the ground. He wrote about Lochnagar, the mountain that made him his victim, about mist in the gullies, deer and ptarmigan on the high tops, and winter loosening its grip in springtime.

> Spring – on dark Lochnagar,
> Where we climb in the snow and the sun
> But it sticks in your craw when the cornices thaw
> And deposit you back at square one.

When it was decided to build a new Bachnagairn bridge in Roy's memory the money rolled in. There was no scarcity of volunteers to do the work. I remember Willie Potts, the keeper, pointing out three poles that stretched across the gap under the old bridge. At one time, that was all that lay between the walker and an icy plunge into the Esk. Now the bridge itself had outlived its usefulness. 'It's defying the laws of gravity,' said Jimmy Nicoll, one of Roy's closest friends and a member of the Tayside mountain rescue team. We were joined by Jimmy Mackie, who had just helped to manhandle a massive block and tackle up the hill from the bogie so that they could put four 32-ft-long steel beams across the gap. Jimmy's name reminded me of two lines from one of Roy's poems:

> Nicky Nacky – Nicky Nack Noo,
> He climbs wi' Tait and Mackie too.

I saw the bridge's progress from time to time and once, when I asked how long it would take to build it Jimmy Nicoll clasped his hands together, turned his eyes to the heavens and said with a smile, 'My friend's up there.' Well, maybe he was right, for the bridge was completed and they all gathered at Bachnagairn to celebrate the official opening. I had an invitation to be there, but I was abroad at the time. The last time I was at Bachnagairn you could scarcely move for walkers sitting around the bridge eating their sandwiches. I wondered if Roy Tait's memorial had opened the floodgates. Maybe there was something to be said for three poles and a prayer...

When I was climbing the windy heights of Bachnagairn some years ago I had the ghost of an old stalker on my heels. This was the way Allan Cameron had come in the nineteenth century, up from his home at Moulzie to cover the Bachnagairn beat of the Glenmuick forest, which later became part of the royal forest of Balmoral. He did it for over forty years, winning himself an unrivalled reputation as a stalker and a notable shot. He knew Queen Victoria, stalked and talked with kings and generals, and was known by stalkers and shepherds, lairds and loons, keepers and cyards – tinkers who came with their 'cairties' to the door of his house at Moulzie.

Allan was following a tradition set by his father, who was head stalker at Glenmuick. He was born in the cottage at the Linn of Muick in 1882. When he was a boy the road outside his house was no more than a hill-track used by shepherds and drovers heading for the Capel Mounth and Glen Clova, but in summer a number of carriages and brakes carried tourists up the glen to the Linn and to Loch Muick, forerunners of the endless stream of traffic using the road today. On one occasion young Allan saw a carriage drawn by four horses stop near the falls on the other side of the Muick. Three ladies stepped down, one of them a small, plump elderly person dressed in black. It was Queen Victoria – and Allan rushed home to tell how he had sighted a 'royal'. Not many years later, his work was to bring him into contact with royals almost every day as he worked his way up from beater to dog-boy, pony-man, ghillie, gamekeeper and under-stalker.

The path from Bachnagairn to Loch Muick runs round the slopes of Broad Cairn, which isn't as broad as the name implies, and goes on to the Sandy Hillock Huts, or what is left of them. The royals used to keep their ponies there when out shooting; and probably still do. From the Hillocks there is a choice of routes to Loch Muick: one is by a steep, narrow path going down to the head of the loch by Corrie Chash, but it can be slippery in bad weather. John Robertson, former stalker at the Spittal of Glenmuick, said that it was a dangerous path when there was a lot of snow, but only one person had fallen off it, and he had been a soldier – a Commando. The second route down to the loch is by a Land-Rover track which runs along the edge of the Loch Braes, opening up a spectacular view of Glen Muick. From there it zigzags down to the Black Burn to join the Capel track.

I have often sat on the edge of that plateau looking down the long shimmer

5.2 Reflections on Loch Muick

of Loch Muick, down to where the river breaks away from the loch and
sweeps past the Spittal and the ruins of Teetaboutie, where an inn once served
travellers going south by the Capel Mounth. There, you are looking into the
heart of the Queen's Country. Across the loch the high lands roll away to the
Little Pap and Meikle Pap (locals rightly call it the *Muckle* Pap), while behind
them is Lochnagar, where Roy Stewart 'climbed in the snow and the sun'
before the mountain claimed him. To the east, the waters of the Allt an Dubh
loch pour down from the dark pool that gives it its name, a drop of almost
800 ft in less than two miles.

Below where I sat a square of windblown woodland could be seen bordering
the track that runs from the Spittal to the Black Burn. It is known as the
Lochend Wuid, and it was on the shore there that the Lochend bothy once
stood. It was a popular and well-used bothy, a centre for climbers and walkers
heading for Lochnagar and the Creag an Dubh Loch cliffs, but it became a
target for vandals, ended up as a terrible eyesore, and had to be demolished.
No lessons were learned from that long-ago episode, for hill bothies are still

under threat from mindless wreckers, and some have had to be closed. Across the water, a track meanders along the lochside on its way from Allt na guibhsaich to the Glas-allt Shiel. When Queen Victoria was at the Glas-allt in September 1850, a new road had been made – 'an excellent one it is', she wrote in her journal, 'winding along above the lake'.

The shiel was built by the Queen in 1868. It stands on a tiny, tree-covered delta which the Prince Consort often visited when he was alive, and it was, as the Queen said, her Widow's House. Thoughts of Albert made her sad, but the Glass-allt also signified a new beginning. 'It is better to have built a totally new house,' she said. They drank whisky toddy at the house-warming, danced 'animated reels', and after Victoria had gone to bed the men went on singing in the steward's room long into the night.

In the past, I have often peered through the windows of the Glass-allt Shiel. Nowadays, walkers are directed round a detour that takes them away from the royal howf, but when there are no royals in the shiel many of them stick to the old route. I remember seeing Victorian paintings on the wall of one of the rooms and pictures of deer on the hills. 'There is a wonderful deal of room in the compact little house,' the Queen wrote in her journal. On the night of the house-warming, or 'fire-kindling', there were nineteen people staying there. The Queen described how they were accommodated. On the upper floor, for instance, there were 'three rooms for Brown, the cook, and another servant', while below were the Queen's sitting room, bedroom, and maids' room. Outside at the back were 'good stables and the keeper's cottage, where our ghillies sleep'.

I half expected to see Sandy Campbell's name on the list, but there was no mention of it. He must have been in the keeper's cottage, for Sandy was stalker at Glass-allt when Allan Cameron was a lad. Young Allan called him Uncle Sandy, although he had a *real* Uncle Sandy – Alexander Cameron. Cameron was stalker at Alt-na-giubhsaich from 1878 to 1905 and when he retired the Cairngorm Club presented him with a gold watch in acknowledgement of 'his unfailing courtesy to all mountaineers who passed through his gate on the way to Lochnagar'.

Sandy Campbell sported a magnificent beard. Queen Victoria didn't like it and asked him to remove it. She said she liked all her stalkers and ghillies to be clean-shaven. But Sandy refused to part with his beard, saying he had never shaved all his life and didn't intend to start now. He told the Queen that he would rather go back where he came from. The matter was quietly dropped and Sandy and his beard stayed at Balmoral. The Campbell family were involved in another domestic crisis, not about beards, but about false teeth! It happened when the ghillies' ball was held at the end of the Balmoral season. Princess Alice, Countess of Athlone, told the story in her memoirs. 'On one occasion old Miss Campbell of the Glass alt Shiel on Loch Muick had told us she could not go to the ball because she had all her teeth out. However, to my surprise she turned up and as I greeted her she explained that she had borrowed a set of false teeth from Miss Cameron of Alt-na-Guithasach Shiel.'

Sandy Campbell was a favourite with Queen Victoria. In his years at Loch Muick he met many members of the Royal Family and their VIP guests, but he was probably known as much for his hobbies as he was for his skill as a stalker. He dabbled in taxidermy in an age when 'stuffers' were much in demand (see chapter 13). The animals and birds he stuffed were put on display, along with other curios, in the Glassallt Shiel's coach-house – 'the Loch Muick Museum', Princess Alexandra called it. Stones found in the hills, cairngorms, quartz, pieces of rock-crystal and rock-salt, deer antlers and the horns of sheep and goats, foxes' masks and brushes – they all found their way into the museum. I never discovered what happened to Sandy's collection in the Loch Muick Museum. If it had survived the years it might have found a place in the visitors' centre at the Spittal.

'He was a bit of an eccentric,' said John Robertson. He planted honeysuckle away out towards the Dubh Loch, halfway between it and the Glass-allt, beside a cairn of stones. He also planted holly trees along the lochside. John thought that only two of them had survived Today, the museum has gone and everything in it, but if things had been different Sandy might have been remembered by one of the cairns he would put up at the drop of a hat. 'If he parted company with somebody,' said John, with a grin, 'he would build a cairn.' He erected one at the lochside and called it Campbell's Cairn, but his self-made monument was demolished by an avalanche about 1957.

Three or four miles north of the Spittal, where the Allt-an-t-Sneachda ('the snowy burn') runs into the Muick not far from the Linn, a dusty track climbs away to a hill called Drum Cholzie. The name always intrigued me, because one interpretation of it is 'the ridge of Acholzie'. My wife's forebears came from the farm of Aucholzie, so I finally went up the track chasing ghosts, noting the names on the map – Creag Dearg, 'the red hill', Fasheilach, 'the hill of the willow bog-stream', Allt an Uisge, 'the whisky burn', and bang in the middle of them all a hill called the Hunt Hill.

It was only later, when I was reading the late Colin Gibson's book, *Highland Deer Stalker*, that the name *Hunt* Hill assumed some significance, for the book described an old-style deer drive that had taken place on the moors around Drum Cholzie. The drive was a combined shoot between Balmoral and Glenmuick, with the Prince of Wales (Edward VII) leading the Balmoral party and Lord Glenesk heading a contingent from Glenmuick House. The prince was placed opposite the junction of the Snowy Burn and the River Muick.

More than 100 beaters met at the Linn of Muick, all armed with flags. They climbed up by the Allt Cholzie towards Creag Dearg and, gathering on the ridge of the hill, went forward with their flags waving. Hundreds of deer were driven down into Glenmuick between the Linn and the ford at Inchnabobart, but the end was farcical. Two shots rang out, two stags fell, and the whole herd broke through the line of beaters and vanished. 'In a minute,' wrote Gibson, 'deer were everywhere on the slopes of Hunt Hill, bounding away towards the skyline. With so many guns and beaters involved, and only two deer shot, this experimental drive was written off as a failure.'

Edward's taste for deer driving came from his father, the Prince Consort, who at Osborne introduced an idea from Coburg known as 'a drive in the old style'. This meant herding a deer into a stockade and then shooting them down from a raised stage. The Queen was invited to watch this 'sport', which brought outraged cries of 'massacre' from the public. His sporting activities in Scotland did little to improve his image, for it was said that deer were driven past the windows at Balmoral so that Albert could take pot-shots at them. When he shot nineteen deer in one day on the moors, some anonymous poet wrote this verse:

> Then from the scene that viewed his warlike toils
> The blood-stained victim hastens with his spoils,
> And laid them humbly at Victoria's feet –
> To such a Queen most intellectual treat.
> So on the grassy plot – to a shambles changed –
> The gory things were scrupulously ranged
> Before the windows of the Royal Guest,
> Famed for the woman softness of her breast.

This was a reference to a ritual which took place after a day's shooting. The stags which had been shot were laid out in front of the castle, including those shot by the 'blood-stained victor', Prince Albert. After dinner, the Queen and her guests came to the door of the castle to see these gory trophies, which were seen under the light of torches held by the stalkers. Whisky flowed, toasts were made and the celebrations went on long after the Queen had gone inside. This is how she described it in her journal:

Bertie shot a stag – a great delight – which was shown by torchlight after dinner, and then the men danced a wild Reel, shouting, carrying the torches in their hands.

Deer driving had gone out of favour when the Prince of Wales became king, but he made an effort to revive it with what was the last deer drive on Lochnagar. The setting was the moors to the south and east of Lochnagar. About 120 beaters gathered at the Glass-alt, setting out from there up by the Dubh Loch to Cairn Taggart, then stringing out over the White Mounth table-land before sweeping the deer before them. Deerhounds were sent down towards the Dubh Loch. Other beaters went up by the Glass-allt waterfall and spread over the moors to close the door into Monelpie Moss. The King's 'butt' was a rock overlooking the Broad Cairn pass and this was the escape route that most of the deer took. The King was happy – he brought down eight stags and the others had six between them.

The King's enthusiasm for deer drives lay behind the building of the path that climbs up Corrie Chash, sometimes known as the Streak of Lightning. John Robertson told me that it was made by Edward in 1903–4. Charlie Bain, a contractor at Ballater, got the job of doing it. It was called the New Walk, but, in fact, it was not a proper walk at all. It was never meant to be used as a path, but was built so that King Edward had easy access to the plateau for deer driving. 'There is no path when you get to the top,' said John. Climbing up Corrie Chash or coming down from the Sandy Hillock Huts, I have often wondered why the path disappeared at the top of Corrie Chash, leaving a stony waste between the so-called New Walk and the Sandy Hillocks track. Now, at last, I knew.

When I went to see John Robertson at his home in Crathie, which he built for his retirement twelve years ago, I learned that his house was called Juniper Lea. It was certainly an appropriate name, for there were juniper bushes all round the house, and when I saw them I couldn't help thinking about the eccentric Sandy Bell. Sandy liked a dram (whisky was half a crown a bottle in those days), but whenever he opened a new bottle he added something to give it a good flavour – juniper berries. 'We'll hae a glass o' the juniper,' he would say.

John's house stands on the edge of an old road leading to the suspension bridge over the Dee. It was a vital link with the South Deeside road when it ran through the grounds of Balmoral Castle to the old Invercauld bridge. There were three generations of Robertsons working as stalkers at the Spittal of Glenmuick. The first was John's grandfather, also John, who came to the Spittal in 1884. He died of measles in 1902, when in his forties, and his son James started working as a stalker when he was 'only a loon of fourteen'. He was there all his days apart from the First World War and retired in 1953. John himself, the third generation, was stalker at the Spittal for thirty-five years.

Hanging in the room I was in were wall plates depicting wartime aircraft. One of them was a Spitfire – the aircraft he flew when he was a pilot in the Second World War. When he was demobbed he came back to the hills, back

5.3 *The Bridge of Dee at Invercauld*

to stalking; he told me it was the freedom of the hills that always appealed to him. There were also two hill pictures in the room: one was a well-known painting by Willie Forbes called 'The Drookit', showing a pony-man splashing through a stream with a dead deer over the pony's back. The other was a painting of the original stalker's house at the Spittal, with Lochnagar looming darkly in the background. John told me it was painted by a mason in 1910. The painter was a drunkard who painted just enough to get himself a drink.

John remembered the old house, which he lived in until it was knocked down in 1928. That year – 'a terrible summer of rain' – they had to move out of the house and into a barn until the house was built. It was decided to build the new house using as many stones as they could from the old one. 'I remember the day it was supposed to start,' said John. 'It was a bonny day, beautiful sunshine, and then the heavens opened.' He never got started. It stayed like that right up to October, and then the house was built in two weeks.

We sat in Juniper Lea and talked about the old days – and about the keepers John had known. The man who probably stood highest in his estimation was Allan Cameron, who had been a second father to him. 'I spent more time on the hill with Allan than I did with my own father,' said John. He was

5.4 *'The Drookit' by Willie Forbes*

a young lad then and must have learned many of his stalking skills from Cameron, who was noted for his marksmanship – 'a tremendous gun' was how John described him. The conversation drifted to Moulzie (locally pronounced Moolie), and it turned out that John's wife Margaret came from Glen Clova. Her father was Hugh Cameron, a keeper in Glen Clova, and it was there that John and Margaret first met.

We spoke about Mabel Gordon, formerly housekeeper to the present Queen Mother at Birkhall, whom I knew. Her father was Frank Gordon, head stalker at Glen Muick; I remember seeing a photograph which hung on the wall of Mabel's house at Blacksmith's Cottages, off the Birkhall road, showing Frank Gordon hauling in fishing nets on Loch Muick, helped by King George V and the Duke of York, later King George VI. They were up to their knees in water. I told John I had seen a similar picture in which half a dozen keepers were doing the same thing, but they were wearing kilts. 'I've been involved in that,' said John, 'but I didna wear a kilt.' He *had* worn the kilt at other times, but said it was 'no fun in snow drifts – ice all round the bottom of the kilt'.

We talked about Sandy McBeth, who went to Glass-allt after Sandy

Campbell. Big, bearded Sandy used to practice with his rifle by shooting at a large stone across Loch Muick. John Robertson told him it was 'a damned waste o' good bullets and good siller'.

'Don't tell the caillich [old woman],' said Sandy. It was his favourite expression. He was an enormous man, said John, but he was a great gardener, laying out paths at Allt na Guibhsaich (if you look carefully you can still see signs of them) and planting flower borders in front of the house. In those days, there was a deer fence all round Allt na Guibhsaich.

John Robertson has seen immense changes since he first went out with Allan Campbell as a lad. When the last deer drive on Lochnagar took place the deer were driven into Glen Muick from Birkhall, for they were scarce on the Balmoral estate in those days. John's grandfather had deer records going back to the time when he first came to the Spittal. They showed that there were only four to five stags killed in a year. There were always deer at Balmoral, said John, but 'nae great numbers'. You could go into the hills for three days before seeing a stag. Later, when the deer numbers grew, most of them drifting in from Invermark, they became a problem. Now the situation has come full circle, with a significant drop in deer numbers. Like Charlie Wright at the old Brig o' Dee, John thinks that the deer forests have been overshot. 'In the 1950s it was nothing for us to get in about to a herd of over 1,000 stags,' he said. 'Today, you're lucky if you see a herd of more than fifty.'

John Robertson was one of a special breed whose names became bywords in the twentieth century. They were mostly local men, handing down their skills from generation to generation, but now most of them have gone. I was told that the stalkers of today were usually incomers. John said he would never encourage *his* son to go in for stalking. 'You wouldn't be a deer stalker any more,' he said. 'You would just be a deer killer.' He has been retired for twelve years, but he still goes out on the moors. In his home at Juniper Lea he has a memento reminding him of his days 'on the hill'. It is a silver cigarette case, given to him by Prince Charles when he retired. There is the figure of a deer on top of it and inside, inscribed in the Prince's own handwriting, are these words: 'With everlasting gratitude for everything you taught me about the hill and about deer but above all for the kind of companionship which will always remain a treasured memory. Charles, October 1987.'

6

Clachanturn

The hamlet of Clachanturn is little more than a mile from Balmoral Castle. It was in a smiddy there that a blacksmith named George Gillespie made the ornate wrought-iron gates that guard the entrance to the royal estate. That was in 1925, in the reign of George V. For three-quarters of a century the gates have been admired by thousands of visitors, but the man who made them has been forgotten, and little Clachanturn has slipped into obscurity.

But one person has never forgotten the Clachanturn blacksmith – this 'dear old man' who loved children. Gillespie's granddaughter, Alexina Archibald, wrote about him in a manuscript drawn up for *her* grandchildren (see chapter 1).

> My Grandfather George Gillespie made the Balmoral Castle Gates and he was paid £50 for his six months' work. They are really lovely and are painted regularly and always very much admired. King George came down to congratulate him on his excellent work. Grandfather said 'I'm glad you like them, the Factor was only going to give me £45 for them, I am asking £50.' King George said 'If you want £50 then £50 it will be, they are beautiful gates.' Grandfather also made the gates which are above the sunken garden and were made the year I was born (1923). They are very ornate gates with thistles, and well preserved.

Alexina told how her grandfather shod 'lovely Windsor greys' that were used to take the King and Queen to church.

> It was a lovely sight with the outrider wearing a red coat and black top hat. The two horses taking the carriage were lovely with the groom dressed like the outrider and his assistant just as handsome. The King and Queen were well seen in those days as the carriage was open and didn't go so fast as modern day cars. We used to feed the horses with carrots when they came in to be shod. The horses were truly magnificent animals.

Today there are no open carriages taking royalty to church, no more red coats

6.1 *The gates at Balmoral Castle*

and top hats, no more horses to feed. Clachanturn lives in the past, tucked away in an idyllic woodland. In spring and early summer forget-me-nots bloom and white anemones carpet the ground like snowflakes. Here, the outside world seems far away. The only link with it is the grumble of traffic on the road above – the turnpike as they called it when they built it a century and a half ago. The houses, only a handful now, stand on the edge of a track running from Easter Balmoral to Abergeldie Castle. It was once a flourishing hamlet, linked to the north Deeside road by a ford, then by two ferry boats, and in 1834 by a new suspension bridge. At one time it had a school with more than eighty pupils and an annual fair called Feill-ma-Halm-oc.

The pulse of Clachanturn was the blacksmith's workshop where Gillespie made his gates. It was a place where travellers took a break before pushing west to Braemar or downriver to the Muick and Ballater. There were three blacksmiths shoeing horses there at the turn of the century, listed in the 1891 Census as James Mitchell, unmarried, blacksmith and ferrier; Frank Duguid, blacksmith; and James Coutts, blacksmith. Mitchell had his sister Margaret as his housekeeper and there was a 'general servant' called Jane Wilson.

An entry in the 1891 Census hinted at busy comings and goings in Clachanturn. 'Mary Lamond,' it said, 'lodging-house keeper.' Two years later, the writer A. I. McConnochie also indicated in his book *Deeside* that Clachanturn had been a busy community. 'Formerly a large market was held here,' he wrote in 1893, 'and some almanacks publish that it is still held. Almost the only part left of the once populous clachan is a "smiddy". It was formerly a complaint in highland parishes that "since the disuse of arms there is scarcely a tolerable smith to be met with".'

Mary Lamond's lodgers would have been travelling on what was part of the old South Deeside road, which 'entered the Balmoral grounds at Easter Balmoral, a neat little village west of the suspension bridge'. Easter Balmoral, now virtually swallowed up by the Balmoral estaste, was also described by another Deeside writer, John Mackintosh, as a 'beautiful little village'. In his *History of the Valley of the Dee*, Mackintosh said it was mainly erected after Queen Victoria came to Balmoral, but, in fact, it was very much a self-contained community before that. Mackintosh also mentioned 'three or four houses standing at some distance from each other on very fine sites which are usually occupied by some of Her Majesty's officials'. These houses, now occupied by Balmoral staff, stand on the brae leading up to Craig Gowan and the road to Glen Gelder.

The hub of village life in Easter Balmoral was the local shoppie, known as Merchant's, which was run by a Mrs Symon, who was said by the Queen to be 'quite an institution'. Victoria was a regular customer there and mentioned it in her journal. In June 1879, before going south, she noted that she had 'stopped at the door of the shop to wish Mrs Symon good-bye'. Eighteen years later, in January 1897, Mrs Symon was still around, but was said to be 'hopelessly ill'. She seemed to take on a new lease of life in time to enjoy the Jubilee celebrations at Balmoral, but later that year, after the Queen had returned to London, the old lady died. The Queen was at Osborne when she heard the news and wrote in her journal: 'We had found her and her good amusing husband in the village when we first came to Balmoral in 1848 and we built them their new house and their shop. She was quite an institution; and everyone, high and low, used to go and see her.' Mrs Symon and her good, amusing husband were sorely missed, but their successors were less popular.

The Symons are buried inside the ruins of the old kirk in Crathie churchyard. John Symon, described on the stone as 'merchant Easter Balmoral', died in July 1876, at the age of sixty-two. His wife, Christina, outlived him by twenty-two years and died in January 1895, at the age of eighty-four. Three of their family died in childhood; James at the age of three and a half years,

Helena aged two and a half, and Victoria aged seven. The sisters, who were said to be 'inveterate robbers', were Maria Isabella and Anne. Both died in 1925 in their seventies.

The South Deeside road was a commutation road up to the 1840s. These roads were maintained by statute labour exacted from farmers and house-holders; the system was oppressive and unsatisfactory and was often evaded, so much so that in the late eighteenth century heritors who were sloppy about calling out their tenants for road work were warned that 'measures for enforcing the performance of the same' might be taken. Eventually, statute labour was commuted for a stated money payment. The commutation roads on Deeside were said to be the best in Scotland up to the period of the turnpikes.

The Act of Parliament giving the go-ahead for a turnpike along the south side of the Dee was passed in 1842. This new turnpike – the present South Deeside road – extended from the Bridge of Muick at Ballater to the Old Bridge of Invercauld near Braemar, following a route by Abergeldie and Balmoral. If it had been left to follow the Balmoral route the face of Upper Deeside might have been vastly different today, but that never happened. In 1857, events took a turn that sent a cold wind of uncertainty down the river. Prince Albert decided to close the road to the public, or, at any rate, that section of it that ran through the royal estate, which meant in the official jargon of the time that the road 'ceased to be'. In other words, six miles of the new South Deeside road was to all intents and purposes wiped off the map and the road ended at Easter Balmoral (see chapter 2).

Two new bridges had to be built so that traffic could be diverted to the North Deeside road, one an iron bridge from Crathie to Balmoral, replacing the suspension bridge, the other at Invercauld, taking over from the Old Brig, which was retained in the royal estate. It was said that the road was being closed because 'the Continuance of it for public use would lead to the Evasion of the Tolls'. Nature shed tears for the old road on the day it closed – the rain fell.

The section of the road no longer open to the public was described in detail in the Act of 1855. It extended from 'the South Dee Side Road at the House occupied by James Smith near the Eastern Boundary of Easter Balmoral in the Parish of Crathie to the South End of the Stone Bridge of Dee called Invercauld Bridge'. The house that James Smith lived in was beside the local hall. Whether or not he approved of the new turnpike stopping at his doorstep is not recorded, but it was from there that I set out to find the 'forgotten' hamlet of Clachanturn.

There are two cottages near the hall. I was told that a souter had lived there at one time. From the hall I followed a track – the old South Deeside road – which ran downhill to the Crathie–Ballater road, then picked itself up on the other side and pushed on to the East Lodge at Abergeldie Castle, a distance of some two miles. Across the Dee I could see Tomidhu, where Betty Grant lived, and to the east the ruins of old settlements that had spread across the Micras. I explored these old ferm touns when I was researching my book, *Land of the Lost*. There were the remains of vanished settlements in the woods around me; the lintel of one old house decorated a garden at Clachanturn. The hamlet lies about halfway between Easter Balmoral and Abergeldie Castle. Its name, like many old place-names, has been spelt a dozen different ways over the years, from Clachinturn in 1607 to Clachanturn, Clachenturn and Clach-an-durn. I found an unusual version in the Valuation Roll for 1859–60 – two farms and a croft called Clachantwin.

The place-name experts had different thoughts on the meaning of the name. James Macdonald, in his *Place Names of West Aberdeenshire*, said it came from *Clach an t-suirn*, the 'stone of the kiln', which may have meant that the hamlet was built on the site of a kiln. William M. Alexander, in his *Place Names of Aberdeenshire*, half-agreed with the kiln theory but said it might be from *an tighearn*, 'of the laird'. Well, you pay your money and take your choice, for there *is* a laird and there *was* a kiln, marked on an 1867 map.

6.2 *Clachanturn, with the smiddy in the centre of the picture*

6.3 *Dawn Williams stands below the tall smiddy lum*

In the huddle of houses that make up the present-day Clachanturn I half expected to find a heap of rubble where the 'smiddy' had been. Instead, Rick Anderson, a former offshore worker living in the West Lodge, pointed to a nearby building. The smiddy was still there, near Clachanturn House, which was occupied by Gareth Williams, another oil worker, and his wife Dawn. Outside, a tall 'lum' rose above the smiddy. Inside, you took a step into the past. Much of it was still as it had been, perhaps even as far back as the time when James Mitchell was shoeing horses. There were two great smiddy fires and tree trunks which had held the anvils, while a heavy hammer and a pair of big, old-fashioned tongs lay nearby. A row of nails on the wall was where the horseshoes had been hung and here an elegant touch had been added to some of the nails; their turned-up tips had been decorated with tiny *fleur-de-lis*, a gesture, perhaps, to the gentlefolk at Balmoral and Abergeldie. Inside that dark old smiddy the fires were cold and dead, but I could almost feel the heat, hear the clang of metal on metal and see the sparks fly. Outside, Rick and Gareth showed me half-hidden landmarks that were links with the Clachanturn of a century ago. Beside the entrance to the West Lodge was a huge stone with what looked like a rusting metal handle on it. This was where the gentry had tethered their horses. Nearby was an old lamp standard, a 'street light' for the road through Clachanturn. Five big beech trees hugged each other inside a circle built of earth and stone. This was a turning point which people used when they arrived in their carriages, sweeping round the circle after dropping their passengers at Clachanturn House.

Generations of Clachanturn blacksmiths had shod horses for travellers, for local farmers, for the lairds, and for royalty at either Balmoral or Abergeldie Castle. Rick Anderson was told that Queen Mary often stopped for a cup of tea at the West Lodge on her way to Balmoral from Abergeldie Castle, which was leased from the Gordons.

I remembered Donald Grant, whose father was host at the Inver Inn in the 1920s (see chapter 9), telling me that when he was a boy he often went to the smiddy at Clachanturn with his father to have their horses shod. Two brothers called McLean had a smiddy at Piperhole on the Tomintoul road, but the innkeeper preferred to walk the extra miles to the Clachanturn smiddy. They were there on one occasion when a ploughing match was taking place and Donald's father decided to have a go at it. 'He was the worst ploughman on the field,' said Donald. 'He got the booby prize – a chunty [chamber pot]!'

Annie Macdonald, the daughter of one of Clachanturn's blacksmiths, served under Queen Victoria and formed a close and lasting friendship with her. Her father was William Mitchell, whose son James and daughter Margaret were mentioned in the 1891 Census. James took over the smiddy when his father died in 1878 at the age of seventy-seven. He himself died in March 1908, when he was sixty-nine, and tragically Margaret, who had acted as his housekeeper, died twelve days later. She was sixty-one. James and Margaret share the same memorial stone in Crathie kirkyard, but Annie, who died in

July 1897, is remembered by a separate stone erected by Queen Victoria.

Annie featured in a will in which Queen Victoria wrote out the names of people she wanted to be reunited with after her death. 'Good John Brown' was on the list – and 'good Annie Macdonald'. They were the only non-royals chosen for this heavenly reunion. Annie had been born at Carn-na-Cuimhne, on the north side of the Dee, in 1832; she was married to John Alexander Macdonald, who was Queen Victoria's footman, for fifteen years. She was in the queen's service for forty-one years, thirty-one of them as wardrobe maid.

Her memorial stone describes her as 'a faithful servant and devoted friend to the Queen'. Wherever Victoria went, her wardrobe maid was never far away; it was on the royal train that Annie got stuck in a dressing room at Keith, with John Brown trying to open it with 'all his might'. At Inverlochy she had a room 'all narrow and long' next to the queen's, and she was with the queen when they drove through Newtonmore. Annie's late husband came from there, but she had never seen the place.

It was Annie who consoled Victoria when Albert died, putting her to bed on the night of his death. In the Queen's Diamond Jubilee year Annie herself was ill, too ill to go to London for the celebrations. In the end she went home to Clachanturn, where she died on 4 July 1897, aged sixty-five. Queen Victoria was greatly distressed. 'I have lost not only an excellent and faithful maid, but a real friend,' she said.

It was from Dawn Williams that I learned about another Annie from Clachanturn – Annie Bey. The Beys were the last blacksmiths at Clachanturn: Edward Bey is dead now, but his widow, Annie, lives in Ballater. Her son Eddie, from Huntly, was there when I visited her and it turned out that he had worked with his father at Clachanturn. He told me he had been smithying since he was a lad. The Beys were thirty years at Clachanturn and thirty years 'doon the road' – meaning the East Lodge at Abergeldie, where they went after leaving Clachanturn. Edward had worked for a wood merchant who took over the smiddy, but he had been in the job for only six weeks when his employer was killed in an accident at Cambus o' May. The local farmers wanted him to stay on, but he had to split his work between the castle and the smiddy. He did shoeing for trekking schools, for Mar Lodge and for Balmoral.

Annie told me that they shod horses for the royal family for forty years, both at Balmoral and at Abergeldie. They had many memories of the 'royals', of Elizabeth and Margaret coming to the smiddy with their horses, of how they made swings for the royal children, and of the time Margaret gave one of the keepers her doll's house to use as a 'garage' for his motor bike. They called the suspension bridge up the road the Auld Brig. Now a footbridge, it was wider at one time, taking horses and carts over the river, but the bridge was eventually narrowed to use only as a footbridge. Over the water at Tomidhu,

Betty Grant's father took his horses across the suspension bridge to the smiddy.

The big house at Clachanturn was occupied for a time by a lady-in-waiting. It had nine rooms, but one was kept for Queen Victoria. Wandering about the house outside the smiddy, I saw an old school bench lying against a wall. It reminded me that Clachanturn once had a school with more than eighty pupils. Three centuries ago, most of the schools were run by the Society for Propagating Christian Knowledge, founded in 1707. There were Society schools at Aberarder, Inverey and Balmoral, and one at Clachanturn about 1720.

The life of a schoolmaster in those far-off days was not a happy one. When the parish school in Crathie closed down after 'some years of struggling existence', the cause was said to be 'the miserable payment given to the schoolmaster'. The Clachanturn schoolmaster, John Young, had more than his 'miserable wages' to worry about. He sent a petition to the minister and kirk session of Crathie Church complaining about interference from 'priests and trafficking papists'. His petition drew a grim picture of a dominie's life in Upper Deeside in the early eighteenth century. Parents wanted their sons to work on the croft instead of sitting at a school desk. When Young went to see them, arguing that younger children who weren't wanted for work should be sent to school, he was told that 'their beasts were so feeble owing to the want of fodder, so that every beast needed a herd or keeper and the young children were wanted for that'. He tried to get backing from 'the much renowned lairds of Abergeldie', but without success.

The Rev. John McInnes, who was a kind-hearted man, rebuked the parents from his pulpit, with the result that there was a slight increase in attendance. But, said the schoolmaster, in November and December there were 'great rains' that prevented the scholars from attending. They were unable to get over the 'flood of water' and when they did Young was forced to send them home again because he 'had not a school nor dwelling-house wherein there was one square yard dry'. Young's own house had water a foot high over the floors. He had to lay 'great stons and feall' (turf) on them and walk over them as if he was crossing a burn.

Summer, harvest and winter rains, said Young, endangered their health, and on top of that 'the Society's books were all damnified and ruined with the rain and water from above and below'. He again went to the honourable lairds of Abergeldie, but with no more success than before. A few well-wishers said they would bring in straw to thatch his house, but there was not enough to cover it. Finally, he appealed to the Presbytery in Kincardine O'Neil and to the Society so that he could be 'eased of the grievances that would render him, or any other Master, useless'. There is nothing to show that he ever received any redress for his losses and misfortunes.

I left Clachanturn with its memories and climbed up a track that seemed to have been 'damnified' by recent rain. The track ran out on the South Deeside road, but continued on the other side of it, opening up striking views of the countryside around Abergeldie Castle and the Mains of Abergeldie. I was looking down on Gordon country. The same family of Gordons have owned Abergeldie since 1481. Alexander, the fourth of his line, was the laird who built the castle. He was known as 'Black Alister' and was heavily involved in the bitter feud between the Gordons and Forbeses.

It was once said that there was not a castle on Deeside, inhabited or habitable, that could compare with Abergeldie. 'There is not even a ruin that raises its head much above a grassy mound that can boast an origin so remote,' was the reported comment of one authority on the antiquities of Aberdeenshire. Oddly enough, although it sits in the heart of what is known as Castle Country, this ancient fortalice, with its square tower, crow-stepped gables and elaborately corbelled turret, is virtually unknown to the public. The Gordons of Abergeldie have never been tourist-minded.

If the castle had boasted a moat and drawbridge the Abergeldie lairds would probably have hauled the drawbridge up to keep out tourists. As it happened, they had a suspension bridge, linking the castle with the north bank of the Dee, and they allowed it to fall into ruin. The bridge was built in 1885. Before that there was a rope and cradle bridge which was one of the sights of Deeside.

For many years the castle was rented to Queen Victoria. Her mother, the Duchess of Kent, lived in the castle for some time, and the Empress Eugenie, widow of Napoleon III, was resident there. It eventually became the Deeside home of the Prince of Wales, the future King Edward VII, who preferred it to Birkhall. Lindsay Smith, who runs the Lochnagar Leisure Shop in Ballater's Station Square, showed me a photograph of the castle as it was during Queen Victoria's lease: a line of buildings can be seen to the east of the castle, grafted on to the square tower. When the lease ended, these buildings had to be demolished, for the agreement was that the castle had to be returned to the Gordons exactly as it was before its royal residents moved in.

I climbed away from the castle, heading for Balnacroft, which I was to explore later, and on to the intriguingly named Khantore, where a path would take me out to the moors which spread away to the Muick. Khantore, which is given in old maps as Kintore, like the Donside village, has its roots in the Gaelic *Ceann Torr*, meaning 'the end of the hillock'.

I remember Annie Bey telling me that she used to see carts coming down from Khantore and crossing the Dee at the Clachanturn ford. It must have been a bumpy ride. The end of the hillock was also the end of the woodland, or almost, for another rough path took me to a high deer fence which separated woodland from moorland. On the way there I passed a track branching off to the left. It was rough and overgrown, with a broken gate, but there was no indication as to what lay at the end of it. I was to find out later when searching for a cottage I had been told about – a house with two front doors. Meantime, I pushed on to the deer fence, where a proper locked gate barred my way, although there was a wooden stile to take me over it. A short distance from the fence was a cairn: not the untidy heap of stones that some hill-walkers throw up for no reason at all, but a well-built cairn. There was nothing to show who raised it or why.

The track curved away through the heather to a road that led to Inchnabobart. Away to my right I could see another cairn, a mighty one, perched on the summit of Craig Lowrigan. It was the pyramid, thirty-five feet high, raised in memory of Prince Albert by his 'broken-hearted widow'. Lochnagar glowered across the moor at me, its dark corries still streaked with the last of the winter snow. Through binoculars I could see tiny figures on the summit. Away to the west was Balmoral Castle. That was where I was going, not to the castle itself, but to Easter Balmoral, where Albert had put up the shutters on inquisitive tourists back in 1857. I wondered what he would have thought of it now. I tipped my hat to him, jumped off the stile, and headed for the Inchnabobart road, where I followed the tang of *usquebaugh* to the distillery, then down to James Smith's house.

7

The Genechal

When I tramped down the dusty road from Easter Balmoral to Inchnabobart some years ago, heading for Glen Muick, I looked across the moors to where a house could be seen half-hidden in an area of thick woodland. The house was shown on Ordnance Survey maps as the Genechal, a name that came from the Gaelic *Sean-choille*, meaning 'the old wood'. That was how local people saw it. From the distance it looked like any other house, but there was one important difference – it had two front doors!

It was a long time before I found out why. One room in the house had been set aside for Queen Victoria, who used it as a 'retreat' when royal shooting parties were out on the moors. When the weather was bad the royal hunters would have their picnic lunch there. Tenancy of the house was given to a crofter family on condition that this room – it had to be a front room – was always made available for use by the Queen, who entered it by one of the two front doors.

The name Genechal has a bold, martial ring to it, almost as if this was some stronghold built to guard the hills and moors around it, not a simple cottar house. In comparatively recent years, the area was treeless, with the Genechal out on the open moor. This was because Canadian lumberjacks stripped the area of its trees during the war. Now, half a century later, the maps are out-of-date, for Sean-choille is living up to its name again. Replanting has thrown a fresh 'plaid' across the hills – and a new wood has grown around the Genechal.

Time has treated the old cottage harshly. In the summer of 1999, a tractor rumbled out of the woodland pulling behind it a trailer packed with slates. They had taken the roof off the Genechal, carrying the slates away to use on farm buildings at Littlemill. I went back there to have a last look at Queen Victoria's hideaway before weather or man and his machines brought it down, for this abandoned building seemed to me to be the symbol of a lost age, standing in a corner of Balmoral that clings more to the past than to the tourist haunts on its doorstep.

The road to Genechal ran through the Old Wood about a mile south of Khantore – a rough, deeply rutted track that seemed to lead to nowhere, then

75

suddenly curved to the right and broke out into open space at the back of Queen Victoria's secret howff. Here, what must have been a larder, built against the rear wall, lay in ruins, its roof gone, its outer walls shattered, wild flowers blooming in the rubble. There were two back doors into the house, but I was looking for two *front* doors. I walked round the house and there they were, side by side – one for the Queen, one for the crofter.

The trees had closed in on the house, leaving barely enough space to walk around it. Nettles rose almost waist high outside the two front doors. The cottage was sturdily built, with thick granite walls. There were only two rooms, with back-to-back fireplaces and a big chimney on the roof above. The door on the left led to Victoria's room, the door on the right to the room occupied by the crofter and his family. Here, there was a hatch in the ceiling leading to wood-lined bedrooms in the loft. Both rooms had pine panelling in Victoria's time, but it had lost its lustre. Long after the Queen had gone her room was papered over and strips of wallpaper still hung forlornly from the wall. The

7.1 *The Genechal today*

back door, which had also been papered, was sealed up. Beside it, a door linking the two halves of the house sagged drunkenly to one side as if someone had tried to kick it in. It was always locked when Victoria was there and the tenants were given strict instructions not to open it.

I found myself in a ghost house, seeing the wraiths of a century ago flitting through those double doors. The floor was thick with dust and rubble. Outside, slates were scattered about the grass as if blown from the roof by winter gales. I could see the sky through great holes in the roof. An ancient swey (a moveable bar over a fire to hold pots and kettles) hung in the shattered fireplace in the crofter's room, while on the other side of the wall was the fireplace where Victoria had warmed herself, perhaps with a dram of John Begg's best in her hand. Through the window I could see a gap in the woods, opening out into a boggy field. Beyond that, nothing but brown moor, stretching away to the distant hills.

The Genechal is a pin-prick on the map. To the south, as far as the eye can see, there is nothing but bare moor and bog, relieved here and there by hills with names like Tom Mor, the 'big hillock', or Tom na h-Olla, the 'hillock of the wool'. To the east is Craig nam Ban, with its tales of witches burned at the stake, and beyond that the ruins of Camlet (An Cam-Leathed, 'the curved slope'), a farm built above Glen Girnock, while to the south the unending wilderness reaches out to the Muick and the Capel Mounth. It was over this bleak terrain that the royal hunting parties took their guns, using the Genechal as a shooting bothy.

Queen Victoria's only mention of the Genechal in her journal comes in an entry describing a shooting trip to the Abergeldie woods with the Prince Consort – and a startling encounter with a 'witch'. Dated 3 September 1849, it reads:

> At a quarter past eleven we drove (the three gentlemen going in another carriage) to the road along which we went with Lord Portman the other days, and up to a small path, where I mounted my pony, Albert and the others walking. We came to *Geannachoil*, and Albert was much pleased with the splendid view. The light was most beautiful, but the heat was overpowering and the sun burning.
>
> We turned to the right when out on the moors, where I got off and walked; and we seated ourselves behind a large stone, no one but Macdonald with us, who loaded the guns and gave notice when anything was to be seen, as he lay upon the ground. The gentlemen were below on the road; the wood was beat, but nothing came, so we walked on and came down a beautiful thickly-wooded glen; and after a good deal of scrabbling to get there and to get up one side of the glen, we sat

down again. We then scrambled over to the opposite side where we again concealed ourselves; in this beat Albert shot a roe.

It is difficult to establish just where the prince made his kill, but the likelihood is that it was at the head of Glen Girnock – the 'beautiful thickly-wooded glen' – where the ground slopes down towards the road to the distillery. Albert, according to the Queen, might have shot a few more deer if it hadn't been for the arrrival of the 'witch'. She described in her journal how the Prince was

> turned back by the sudden appearance of an old woman who, looking like a witch, came along through the wood with two immense crutches and disturbed the whole thing. Albert killed the roe just as she was coming along and the shot startled her very much. She was told to come down which she did, and sat below in the glen, motionless, having covered her head with her handkerchief. When two of the beaters came down and were told to take up the roe, they first saw the old woman, and started, and stared with horror – which was very amusing to see. I rode a little way afterwards, and then we seated ourselves behind a bush, in the rear of the wood, close to the distillery.

There the diary entry ends. There is nothing to show whether or not the Queen spoke to the old woman, or where she came from, or what happened to her. You are left with the uneasy feeling that Victoria went off to find another bush, leaving her crippled subject sitting in the broiling sun with a handkerchief on her head.

The Prince of Wales, who preferred Abergeldie to Birkhall, often made use of the Genechal when out shooting on the Abergeldie moors, following the pattern set by Victoria, who had a number of hideaways in houses on both the Balmoral and Abergeldie estates. There was one at Clachanturn House, which was occupied by a lady-in-waiting, and another at Rhebreck, the house of John Grant, the Queen's head forester. The Genechal was the only house where she had her own front door, separating her from the occupants, allowing her to come and go as she pleased. The likelihood is that it was planned and built with two doors or adapted to give the Queen the privacy she always wanted.

The tenants at the Genechal were the McDonalds – George and his wife Margaret. George worked on the royal estate and was given tenancy of the Genechal so that he could combine the job of crofter and caretaker. He wasn't the first to share his house with the Queen; a family of Essons were there before the McDonalds moved in. Jimmy Esson, head of the household, worked at Lochnagar distillery.

7.2 *George and Margaret McDonald*

Lairds and ministers were almost the only people with stone houses at the beginning of the nineteenth century. The crofters' crude homes were built of unhewn stones and mud, thatched with heather or broom, and inside were two rooms divided by wooden partitions. When the Queen and Prince Albert bought Balmoral, Albert set out to replace these 'miserable hovels' (he thought they 'bordered on the Irish') and the Genechal was probably one of the new breed of stone houses built by the Prince Consort.

The crofts or holdings seldom exceeded ten to twelve acres and barely yielded sufficient grain to support the family. Oatmeal and milk were the staple food of the household and the crofters generally possessed a cow. George McDonald's great-great-granddaughter, Winnie Smith, remembers hearing that he had a cow *and* a horse at the Genechal. The horse had a foal, but when they went out to look at it they found it lying on the ground, dead. 'They saw the mark of the mare's foot on her,' said Winnie. 'My Grannie was afa upset about that.'

'Grannie' was Annie Stewart McDonald, granddaughter of George and Margaret McDonald. In a sense, it was through her, in the tales told by *her* grandchildren, that I was able to turn back the years and see the Genechal of more than a century ago. I listened to stories about Queen Victoria's visits to the lonely cottar house. I learned about life at the Genechal and how the McDonalds had lived in only *half* a house, with the other half reserved for the Queen, and how they finally moved to other holdings on the Abergeldie estate, to Tornauran and Khantore and Catanellen, the 'sheep-cot of the streamside field'.

There had been a garden in front of the house. I was shown a picture of the McDonalds' daughter, Chrissie, standing at its gate with the Genechal's double doors in the background, holly climbing up the wall. Years after the old house had been abandoned, its double doors locked to keep out intruders, members of the family would go there on a Sunday to hold picnics and talk about Grannie and the old man. Winnie Smith had a studio portrait of them in their old age. It was taken not long after they had left the Genechal, when the years had stolen up and left its mark on them. George was sitting in a chair in his Sunday suit, his watch-fob dangling from his waistcoat, his neat grey beard falling over his starched white collar. He seemed a frail figure beside his wife, who stood beside him, a shawl over her shoulders, the wide ribbons from her hat tied in a large bow under her chin. Her hair was white and she had a bracelet on her wrist, but her hands were rough from a lifetime of hard work.

I learned about the good years and the bad years, and about how tragedy had marred their lives – a double tragedy in the house with double doors. In June 1898, the McDonald's eldest son, Willie, died at the Genechal; he was only thirty-three years old, in the prime of life. Less than a year and a half later they lost their oldest daughter Elsie – Annie McDonald's mother.

The McDonald women had often walked over the hills from the Genechal to Girnock and thought nothing of it. 'The only thing they were scared of', I was told, 'was when the Camlet bull was on the hill.' Generations of the Kennedy family lived at the Camlet. Records show that in the late nineteenth

7.3 *Chrissie McDonald, at the gate outside the double doors of Genechal*

century it was farmed by a William and James Kennedy. When Elsie McDonald set out from the Genechal to go over the hills to Girnock on a cold December day in 1899 it was to collect potatoes. She returned with a full sack, carrying it all the way on her back. It was her last trip. Not long after that she fell ill and died, and it was said that carrying a heavy sack of potatoes over the hills had been the main cause of her death. She was twenty-nine.

Annie McDonald was eight years old when her mother died. It was left to her grandparents to bring her up, but for them the years were slipping away. George, born in 1836, was sixty-three, Maggie six years younger. A new century was coming in, but the crofter and his wife were trapped in the old one, set in their ways, their children grown up and away from home. They had lost their oldest son Willie; then their oldest daughter, and now they had to think of Annie. It was like starting all over again.

The Genechal was a lonely place for little Annie. There were no other children to play with. Here, the only world she knew was *Sean-choille*, 'the old wood', a green 'plaid' that lay over her shoulders, not like Ballochbuie, which Queen Victoria had said was 'the bonniest plaid in Scotland', but a dark, mysterious place that became her dream world. She would often dance around the trees outside the house, a lonely, solitary figure, whirling and pirouetting like a lady at a ball in the laird's castle. She would lie in bed at night hugging her pillow, hearing the soughing of the wind and the night-time sounds of the wood, wondering if the witches from Craig-nam Ban were afoot. She would lie there, looking out of the skylight window, watching the branches of the trees making figures of eight against the night sky.

She had no toys to play with, so she made a doll out of her pillow. Queen Victoria must have seen her playing with it, or was told about it, for on one of her visits to the Genechal she turned up with a real doll for Annie – a royal doll, not the sort of gift a humble crofter's granddaughter would expect to get, even from a queen. Grannie McDonald certainly thought it too good for her granddaughter, for she took it away from her. It was given to some other child, nobody knows who, or, for that matter, why.

But Elsie's daughter had a good upbringing. Annie was sent to school at Crathie in the summer and to Girnock in winter. If the weather was too bad to go home she stayed with the people who ran the Girnock Post Office. At one time, the school at the Bridge of Girnock was threatened with closure, but it was saved when a new miller called Henry Nicholson was appointed to the Mill of Cosh. He came down from Shetland to take up the post, bringing his family with him: all twelve of them! 'I can remember my mother saying there was one in every trade,' said Lena, Winnie Smith's sister, 'slater, joiner, mason and so on.' At any rate, there were enough to ensure that the school stayed open.

The coming of the Shetlanders was to change Annie McDonald's life, for she grew up and married one of the miller's family, Thomas Nicholson. It was a story that had a sad ending, for in 1918 Annie Nicholson, as she now was, reeled under a blow that was as terrible as the loss of her mother and uncle nearly twenty years before. Tom Nicholson joined the army when the First World War broke out and was sent to France – he never returned, dying of wounds in October 1918. Annie's favourite uncle, John McDonald, also went off to war. He joined the 1st Gordon Highlanders and was killed in action near Romeries, on the same day that Annie's husband Tom died. It was thought that he had been killed by a British shell.

The story of the Genechal is the story of two women; the family still talk about Grannie and Aul' Grannie. Aul' Grannie was Margaret Anderson McDonald, the crofter's wife who shared her house with a queen, and Grannie was Annie McDonald, her granddaughter, who grew up at the Genechal, married Thomas Nicholson and herself became a grandmother. Annie was a happy person, who was rarely seen to be 'ill-nat'rd'. 'She was Gran' tae a'body,' said Winnie.

In the studio photograph taken with her husband, Margaret McDonald looked very much the matriach, which was not surprising for a woman who had reared seven children in a back o' beyond croft. Their names were William, Elsie, John, Alexander, Christine, James and Margaret.

The old woman was said to be a hard worker, but a hard woman as well, with principles as solid as the rock on Tom Buailteach. Annie used to say, 'She didn't let me away wi' onything.' She was hardly ever seen without her Bible – and she wouldn't let you into the house unless you were christened. When she wasn't reading her Bible she was knitting . . . knit, knit, knitting, mostly white socks. A newspaper cutting from the 1930s reported on a sale of work held at Crathie church hall and visited by the queen. 'A pair of socks which won a prize in *The Daily Mail* knitting competition was raffled at the sale,' it read. 'They were knitted by a 91-years-old Crathie woman, Mrs McDonald.'

Two years before the war broke out, George and Margaret McDonald left the Genechal. The old couple moved to Tornauran, a thirty-acre croft with 'rough' land on the road to Lochnagar distillery: local folk called it Torrnywarron. George died there in 1915 at the age of seventy-nine. Their son James took over the tenancy of Genechal in 1911 but later moved to Tornauran, which became the family home. The Genechal stood empty for a time, until Tom Nicholson's brother John and his wife moved in (they later moved to Khantore).

Christina ('Chrissie') McDonald, who never married, went to Tornauran to look after her parents. Chrissie was in royal service at Balmoral and often went south with Queen Victoria to Sandringham and Windsor. Victoria showed her appreciation by giving her a jewellery box inscribed 'To C. McDonald from the Queen'. Chrissie died in 1946 aged sixty-eight. Her brother Alexander (Sandy) died at Tornauran in 1934. Annie, who had lived at Catanellan with her daughter Winnie Nicholson, also moved to Tornauran and died there in 1965 at the age of seventy-five. James McDonald died in 1951; his death broke the McDonald line at Tornauran. The tenancy went to James

7.4 *'Auld' Grannie – Margaret McDonald with her Bible*

Cruickshank, from Foveran in Buchan, who worked at Lochnagar distillery. He married Margaret (Peggy) Nicholson, Annie's daughter, and they had a family of four: Lena, Sandy, Chrissie and Winnie.

So that was the Genechal. The McDonalds, as well as the families they married into, the Nicholsons and Cruickshanks, have always been proud of their heritage. I sat with Winnie and Lena and talked about the Genechal and Aul' Grannie; about how Victoria called at the Genechal on one occasion and discovered that Margaret McDonald was ill. 'Have you got a doctor?' the Queen asked. 'Oh, no,' said Mrs McDonald, she couldn't afford a doctor. 'Well,' said the Queen, 'I'll send up *my* doctor,' adding, 'You'll have a doctor as long as you need one.' Victoria kept her promise – and the patient lived well into her nineties. On another occasion Mrs McDonald was chopping sticks outside her house at the Genechal when Queen Victoria passed. It was raining and the Queen gave her a big parasol with her name carved on the handle. She let her keep it and it stayed in the family for years.

Margaret McDonald was said to be excessively houseproud. She would, for instance, never allow anyone into the parlour. That was the room set aside for the Queen. Today, an old-fashioned dresser stands in the living room of Winnie Smith's house at Leys Farm, near Tarland. It is polished to perfection and it sits there as a reminder of the Genechal days and of how it once dominated the room used by Queen Victoria. There were other mementoes – a Victorian cape, beautifully braided, worn by Margaret McDonald; a silver teapot from the Genechal, snapshots taken outside the cottage, one with Aul' Grannie holding a stick in one hand and a Bible in the other; feathers and flowers pressed inside old books, among them a four-leafed clover. I wondered who had found it and how lucky it had been.

We sat over a huge box of books, all dating back to the late nineteenth century, or the early years of the twentieth century. Two belonged to members of the family who had no four-leafed clover luck. 'Elsie McDonald 1878' was written inside one, while another was a school prize from Crathie School (Crathie*side* School it said). The book was called *Harvey Sinclair* and the inscription on it read, 'A Gift from Her Majesty to John McDonald, July 22, '92.'

Another book belonged to John's brother – 'James McDonald, Genechal Cottage, Crathie, 1907.' The title of that book was *I Will Repay, a Romance 1907* and the author was Baroness Orczy, better known for her novel *A Scarlet Pimpernel*. There was also a newspaper cutting. It showed the Balmoral Highlanders – the Deeside equivalent of the Lonach Highlanders – marching through Braemar in 1928. Stepping out in the middle of them was James McDonald; the uniform which he wore when he was a member of that exclusive band of Balmoral Highlanders is still in the family, including a kilt of Royal Stewart tartan. Queen Victoria said the uniform had to be worn only by Highlanders.

Now the Balmoral Highlanders have gone and the Genechal has gone. The removal of the Genechal's roof in 1999 was a kind of symbolic act, the tearing down of one of the last links with Deeside's Victorian past. Here, on

Balmoral's doorstep, change has come slowly. I was shown a snapshot of the Genechal when the building was still intact. It stood in open space, which could only mean that the picture was taken after the lumberjacks had done their work. Today, Sean-choille, 'the old wood', has reclaimed its own. It is more than likely that in a few years the cottage will have deteriorated. It will no longer be a house with unique double doors – one for the crofter, one for the Queen.

8

The Geldie burn

Up on Tom Buailteach a huge cairn dominated the hill. It matched in size the cairn on the Coyles of Muick, built to commemorate the marriage of the Prince of Wales (later Edward VII) and Alexandra, Princess of Denmark. Local people called it the Prop of the Buailteach, but there was nothing to show who built it, or why. I could see Balmoral Castle in the distance and I wondered if this was one of the cairns scattered about the estate by Queen Victoria to mark royal events like marriages and deaths.

Below me was Lochnagar distillery, where John Begg once supplied Balmoral Castle with whisky 'by the gallon'. He did it for the building of the cairn at Craig Gowan after Victoria and Albert had bought Balmoral. 'Whisky was given to all,' the Queen noted in her journal. I had a fleeting picture in my mind of kilted Highlanders skirling and dancing round the crumbling cairn in Tom Buailteach while *usquebaugh* flowed out of royal casks like water gurgling down the Geldie burn.

The name Tom Buailteach means 'the hillock of the summer huts'. These were shiels used by crofters grazing their cattle on summer pastures and the ruins of some of them could be seen on the lower slopes of the hill. I had come to the Buailteach through the densely wooded Cabrach, where old tracks push through the heather in all directions, some still in use, some barely visible. 'Cabrach' comes from *caber*, 'a place of poles or trees', but it is also a place of hills and hillocks, Tom Buailteach for one, also Tom na Croiche, 'the hangman's hillock', less than a mile from Abergeldie Castle, and Tom an Uird, 'the hillock of the round hill'.

Tom Buailteach overlooks a narrow back road that loops away from the south Deeside road near the Mains of Abergeldie and wanders west to Lochnagar distillery and Easter Balmoral. This was one of the roads that Queen Victoria took when she visited 'poor people and others' living in thatched cottages near Balmoral. On her way, she stopped at the shop at Easter Balmoral to buy them gifts – a dress perhaps, or a handkerchief, or maybe a petticoat. She found it all 'touching and gratifying'.

Time stands still in this quiet backwater, even though the 'thackit' cottages have long since gone and the 'poor people' with them. When I set off along the narrow road I was, I suppose, stepping back in time, following tracks on a map which showed the area as it was a century ago. It was drawn for me by Lena Cruickshank, great-great-granddaughter of George and Margaret McDonald, who lived in the area after leaving the Genechal.

The map showed the Geldie Burn. It rises near Creag nan Gall, which means 'the rocky hill of the foreigners', although who the foreigners were and what story lay behind them I never discovered. Perhaps I was walking in their footsteps, following the Geldie as it gurgled through the Cabrach by the Buailteach and Catanellan on its way to join the Dee near Abergeldie Castle.

There are two Geldie Burns on Upper Deeside. Lena speaks about her area as Glen Geldie, and complains that her burn is ignored by Ordnance Survey maps, unlike the mightier Geldie Burn that runs into the Dee west of the Linn of Dee. On her map, however, the little Geldie Burn is given its rightful place. Its course is followed down through the Cabrach and into the Dee east of Abergeldie Castle.

The old road from Clachanturn to the castle runs parallel to the Dee and is marked on the map as The Avenue. Halfway along it are the Red Stables (they had red roofs) and a group of houses for servants and estate workers. During the war they were filled up with evacuees, and when the war was over the Queen's Guard stayed there instead of being quartered in the Barracks at Ballater. There was a nightly treat for the locals when the guard 'beat the retreat' near the castle. All the buildings have gone, demolished, including two rows of houses straddling a track that broke off from the Avenue and ran down to a suspension bridge across the Dee. The track has more or less disappeared and the bridge, now in a ruinous condition, was closed a number of years ago.

The Geldie Burn, which gives its name to Abergeldie Castle, enters the Dee west of the vanished Red Stables. It formerly supplied water to a defensive moat at the castle. The castle is on the right bank of the Dee, but it was believed at one time that both it and the site of Balmoral were on the left bank. A. I. McConnochie, in his book *The Royal Dee*, said that traces of the old channel of the river were particularly noticeable below the suspension bridge. It is an intriguing thought, for it would have meant that Balmoral Castle would have been on the North Deeside road and the South Deeside road, the old right-of-way through the royal estate, might not have been closed.

During Queen Victoria's long lease of the castle it became the home of her mother the Duchess of Kent. The Empress Eugenie, widow of Napoleon III, was a resident there for a time, but it eventually became the home of the Prince of Wales, the future King Edward VII, and his children. In more recent times it was used to accommodate various guests of the Royal Family while at Balmoral. Garden parties, fêtes and official receptions were held on its lawns.

8.1 *Abergeldie Bridge*

The Mains of Abergeldie is within a stone's throw of the castle entrance. From the road it looks like an untidy clutter of old farm buildings, but the farm itself still carries a hint of faded glory. During Queen Victoria's long lease of Abergeldie, including the Mains, the farm was also used as a kind of annexe to Balmoral, housing prominent members of the court and their wives when the Queen was in residence on Deeside. Harriet Phipps, who was maid of honour to the Queen and later an assistant private secretary, stayed there for a time with her husband, Sir Charles Phipps, the Queen's treasurer.

In 1854 it was taken over by Dr Andrew Robertson, the Queen's commissioner, whose daughter, Patricia Lindsay, described it in her book, *Recollections of a Royal Parish*, as 'little more than an ordinary farmhouse'. From time to time, however, the Queen added to it, and always personally inspected any alterations that were made. 'I maun hae everything snod [tidy] or the Queen comes,' the commissioner's housekeeper, Mary McHardy, used to say, 'for naething escapes her een.'

I was thinking of Mary McHardy when I wandered into the Mains. There were no hens clucking about the yard, and not a cow to be seen in the byre, which would have brought a sharp comment from the housekeeper, for she was also a dairy and poultry woman. She was known to speak her mind, bluntly and forcibly, and some people were a little afraid of her. Even the Queen's commissioner stood in awe of her. The titled visitors who came to stay at the Mains were careful to address her as *Mrs* McHardy, but she tended to scoff at this display of respect from her betters. 'It's Mistress McHardy when the gran' folks are here,' she would say, 'but I'm jist plain Mary again noo.'

Patricia Lindsay drew a lovely word-picture of the crabby old housekeeper. 'Dear old Mary!' she wrote. 'I can see her now enjoying her cutty pipe by the fire in the kitchen, for she was one of the few women-smokers left in our part of the country in my young days. "She couldna dee wintin' her smoke" she used to say, and she could get no more acceptable gift than a packet of the strong-flavoured brown twist to be got at Symon, "the mairchants". Mary was an excellent dairy and poultry woman, and her "beasts" – the term included fowls – must be properly attended to whatever happened to the humans.'

Two distinct communities, Balnacroft and Khantore, are marked on Lena Cruickshank's map, as are the tracks that led to them. One was the track I had taken from Clachanturn to Balnacroft – an old droving route called the Claigionn Road (shown on the map as the Claggan), which went up by Khantore and over the moors to the Spittal of Muick. It runs below Claigionn Mullach, 'a rounded hillock of eminence', but it was apparently not sufficiently eminent to be marked on the map. Now rough and overgrown, the track climbs away from the South Deeside Road and emerges at a row of old houses known as The Street, which joins the road from the Mains of Abergeldie to Lochnagar distillery.

The name Balnacroft – Baile na croite, 'the town of the croft' – suggests a sizeable community and, in fact, the 1861 Census listed fifty-two names in this hamlet. On her map, Lena Cruickshank separated the two communities of Balnacroft and Khantore and indicated the number of children living there in the 1940s and 1950s. There were eighteen in The Street itself, including four in The Kennels, a large house once occupied by a gamekeeper.

The majority of cottages on the Abergeldie estate are let out, mostly to incomers. Mary Summers lives in a 'double' cottage at the end of The Street. There were eight children in these cottages, five in one, three in the other. Mary, who linked them up, could claim to be 'naturalised', an adopted Abergeldite, for she has been there for thirty years. When she came to Balnacroft the cottages were tenanted by old people who had been born and brought up in Abergeldie and could tell you about its people and its past. Now, says Mary ruefully, she is the oldest.

Winnie Smith's aunt, Winnie Nicholson, who now lives in Ballater, was born at Balnacroft – 'just beside Catanellen, not The Street'. This was at Balnacroft Cottage, opposite Catanellen, about half a mile from Balnacroft Farm. Winnie thought that the houses in The Street were occupied by estate workers, not distillery employees, although some people said that The Street had been built for the distillery. The situation is complicated by the fact that

8.2 *The Street*

there was another distillery in the area before John Begg's Lochnagar distillery. A man called William Farquharson opened a small distillery on land let by the laird of Abergeldie, but it 'was not long in use'. It was said to be sited somewhere near Balnacroft Farm and its 'founds' were reportedly seen by workers digging there.

There was little doubt that the folk of Upper Deeside liked their dram, legal or otherwise. 'We used to have a lot o' sma' stills here,' said Winnie. 'A' ower the place!' Their neighbours over the hill in Glen Girnock were just as eager to get their share of *usquebaugh*. As many as a dozen 'black bothies' were said to operate in the upper part of the glen and if you searched long enough and hard enough you might still find the remains of old stills in remote corners of the glen. Early in the twentieth century a local Girnock man recollected seeing a line of thirty horses starting from Strath Girnock, loaded with smuggled whisky *en route* for the south by the Capel Mounth in Glen Muick.

Winnie recalled a Mrs Sim whose father had a still at the bottom of Craig na Ban. This was down at Geldie Cottage, where Willie Sim had a tailor's shop. The cottage sits at the roadside near a track leading up to the Witch's Hill. Two other houses called Abergeldie Cottages lie on that route. The Den and the American Gardens are nearby, but they have nothing to do with Yankee botanists. Adam Watson and Elizabeth Allan give the name as it is pronounced locally – Gairdens, American Gairdens – but the word 'American' is really a corruption of the Gaelic *Meuragan*. The Gairdens, incidentally, are a small patch of trees. Willie Sim lived in Geldie Cottage with Charlie Grey, who had a long white beard, and with them was 'a funny little wifie' called Bella Milne, who was their housekeeper.

Lena Cruickshank's map shows a track breaking away from the Claggan and running parallel with it towards Balnacroft Cottage, while another path goes up to Tom na Croiche, 'the hangman's hillock'. I was told that the top of the hangman's pole could still be seen there and that it had been covered with stones to keep the pole in. I never found this gory relic, for the track had long since vanished and the path up to Tom na Croiche was lost in heavy woodland. The track itself had been a right of way, running up through open fields to the distillery road, passing Balnacroft Cottage, where Annie Beddie lived.

Tornauran Farm, which became the McDonalds' family home, is only a short distance from Balnacroft. It was not as remote or as wild as the Genechal, but life was never easy there in the old days. They could remember winters in which the snow was level with the dykes. There were no snow ploughs and they had to walk from Tornauran to The Street to get loaves of bread, carrying them in keepers' bags.

Tornauran Farm also became a kirk during the Second World War. If you had walked up the distillery road in the early years of the war you might have seen a piece of paper nailed to a tree near the phone box; it carried a message written on the back of a discarded Order of Service notice from Crathie church – 'Afternoon service in Tornauran Farm. Saturday 27th October at 3.30 pm.'

The services were laid on for old folk and other people not fit enough to go to kirk. Twenty people turned up for the first service in 1940 and were crammed into the kitchen. The father of Anne Beddie, who lived in Balnacroft Cottage, had made a pew for them – a long bench laid out against the kitchen wall. Chairs were begged and borrowed. It was an afternoon service, taken by the Crathie minister, Dr Lamb, and it lasted about three-quarters of an hour.

The main approach to Khantore is by a road near The Street, but Lena's map showed me another route, a continuation of the right-of-way from the Claggan, crossing the distillery road and following a track that starts at Catanellen. From there, it runs to the Geldie Burn, then splits in two, one leg going through the Cabrach, the other crossing the burn and pushing on as An Garadh, which means 'a dyke'.

Up on a hillock on the left was Braehead, once a ruin, now beautifully rebuilt by Neil and Katy Beattie, using the old beams. Farther on, the map shows the right-of-way doing a sharp left-hand turn. This takes you to the brae climbing up from Balnacroft Farm to what A. I. McConnochie called 'the little hamlet of Khantore'. The right-of-way here was once used as a short-cut by the local postie, but now it is overgrown and out of use. I left it and carried on up An Garadh, entering Khantore, as I thought, by the back door. To my surprise, I was entering another 'street'.

There were ruins and larachs all along this last stretch of my walk into Khantore, signs of a settlement – a street – that went back long before the street on the Claggan was built. There was little doubt that this was the original Khantore, pronounced Kintore, as in the Garioch burgh. The name comes from *Cean torr*, 'hill end' or 'hill head'. It seemed to be an accurate description when I stood on the brae looking down on the scattered houses that made up this small community.

That was the Khantore of the past. I wondered what sort of people had lived in the primitive houses that now lay along the track in dust and rubble; the Khantore of the present is populated by 'incomers'. It is a word often used in a derogatory sense, but without incomers and 'white settlers' there would be more broken walls and larachs. It was among the 'founds' in the settlement that I met an incomer whose link with the hamlet goes back over many years. Agnes Short, the well-known writer of historical novels, and her husband, Professor Tony Short, became permanent residents at the Khantore farmhouse when he retired. Now, away from the cloistered calm of Old

Aberdeen, Mrs Short does her writing in a study in one of the farm buildings. The Professor is happy there, but finds it a bit nippy in the winter.

Down the hill is Birch Cottage, one of three cottages whose gable-ends nudge each other on the Khantore brae. Dr Dorothy Gibb has had Birch Cottage for forty-two years, but was away a lot of that time doing university work on biology, travelling all over Britain. Up on the breezy braes of Khantore she is in another world. Her retirement has cut her off from the kind of busy life she once had and her only regret is that she doesn't see a lot of people.

She is bright, lively, and animated, with a ready laugh, and her face lit up as we talked. Inside the house the walls were lined with water-colours which she had painted – and sold – until she had eye trouble. She was also a photographer and I was shown many striking landscapes she had taken. Now, although she had an operation which has given her back her normal sight, she doesn't feel like returning to her hobbies.

She also bred horses and had a considerable reputation as a horsewoman. She worked for the Queen Mother during the shooting season, taking cartridges up to the shooting butts and carrying stags off the hill on Highland ponies. Now her horses have gone. The field next to her house where she grazed them lies untouched and the wooden stables where she kept them are empty.

When I was on the Khantore brae I thought in a fanciful way that I might hear the sound of Willie Blair's fiddle come dancing down the years, for the Queen's fiddler lived in one of the three cottages there. His name still means something in this corner of Deeside. Winnie Smith told me about the time her eldest daughter, Angela, played in the Golden Fiddle contest in the Caird Hall, Dundee. Her tutor thought her fiddle wasn't good enough for the competition. 'That's nae a good fiddle tae play in the contest,' he said. 'I'll gae ye this een.' 'This een' was Willie Blair's fiddle. Angela won the Golden Fiddle award with it and later, when she was older, won the senior award with it. She was fourteen when she won the Golden Fiddle award; she is now thirty-two and married.

Willie Blair's house is the lowest of the three on the Khantore brae. It stands opposite the end of the right-of-way path I had been on when tramping up An Garadh – the path once used by the local postie. By an odd coincidence, a former postman now lives in the house. Douglas Fife and his wife came on holiday to Khantore for fifteen years and have lived there for five years; both are Glaswegians. Douglas had a shop in Glasgow, but gave it up and joined the Post Office. He was transferred to Ballater and was postman there for ten years, then he retired. Now he works at Balmoral during the season when the castle is open to the public.

8.3 *Willie Blair's house, with its latticed windows. Mr and Mrs Douglas Fife
live there now.*

The sign outside his house says Druimview. At first it was Drumview, but
Douglas' daughter told him the proper word was Druimview; it was origi-
nally called Balnacroft, but Balnacroft Cottage is nearby and Balnacroft Farm
is down the brae, so Douglas decided to change it. He approached the laird,
John Gordon, who told him that there were two fields beside the cottage called
Big Drum and Little Drum, so that was what he called the house.

The correct name is the Gaelic *Druim*, meaning 'a ridge', but the anglicised
version Drum appears in a lot of place names. There are a number of both
Druims and Drums in *The Place Names of Upper Deeside*. 'The Druims' is
given as a collective name for the Upper and Lower Druims Parks at
Abergeldie, presumably the Big and Little Drums. In James Macdonald's book,
Drumnapark is given as 'a ridge of the park'.

Whatever the name, it certainly has an impressive outlook. I stood with
Douglas and his wife looking out from a window across the fields and beyond
the Dee to the hills above Micras, where ruined settlements lie all along the
hillside. I could see Torgalter, where there was once a small clachan and a

boathouse, which was also an alehouse called Clinkums. To the west a mast for mobile phones rose up above the house where Rab Bain lives in his farm at Ardoch.

Drumview hasn't changed since Willie Blair lived in it in Queen Victoria's time, apart from a small extension for a bathroom and a kitchen. The latticed windows are still there, as is the big open fireplace with the swey and a big black kettle on it. Winnie Smith's grandmother, Annie McDonald, had an aunt, Jean Taylor, who lived in the house. She was a First World War widow, like Annie, and because of that both were given houses on the Abergeldie estate at a nominal rent, a benefit that was never to be altered.

Jean was said to be a 'spooky' woman, always speaking about bad omens and claiming that she had heard the ghost of Willie Blair in the house. Charlie and Peggy Stewart, her nephew and niece, spent their holidays with her at Khantore and then went to live there. They eventually got the house next door, the Firs, to live in. I asked Doug Fife if anyone had actually seen or heard anything 'spooky'. Apparently, Charlie Stewart once said he was in the room upstairs when he heard someone in the house and footsteps coming up the stairs. They stopped outside his room. Charlie opened the door – and there was no one there.

When Queen Victoria visited the people in Balnacroft, she noted in her journal that she had 'peeped into Blair the fiddler's'. Willie, who composed as well as played, was known as the Neil Gow of Deeside. He played at balls and festive gatherings at Balmoral for more than thirty years and was in demand at every ball and festivity in the area, including the ghillies' ball at Balmoral. Patricia Lindsay said he was 'a bit of a wag in a kindly cynical fashion'. He kept a critical eye on the dancers when he played, and on one occasion told a lady that there was not a dancer on the floor like her husband. She was delighted. What he said was true, but not in the sense that she accepted it, for her husband could scarcely put one foot past the other.

Patricia Lindsay said that he was 'so much in social request that over-conviviality was apt to follow'. It was an understatement. The truth was that Willie had two loves – his fiddle and the whisky bottle. The Crathie minister, the Rev. Archibald Anderson, often warned him against over-indulgence. He once went to see the minister after playing at the Inver Inn and told him, 'I've been ower to a dance at the Inver, Mr Anderson, and I jist came in on my wye hame that ye micht see me, in case ye wid hear I wis waur than I am'.

John Brown is said to have drunk at the Inver, so maybe he shared a glass with the Queen's famous servant. It must have been hard for Willie not to succumb to temptation, for over-indulgence was all about him at Balmoral. Sir Frederick ('Fritz') Ponsonby, assistant private secretary to Queen Victoria, said that the amount of whisky consumed by the servants was 'truly stupendous'.

The whole atmosphere was wrong, he declared – 'A drunken man was so common that no one ever remarked on it.'

When John Brown's cousin, Willie Leys, was dismissed for drunkenness in 1876, Sir Thomas Biddulph, Keeper of the Privy Purse, commented, 'The wonder is that these Highlanders are not more often drunk than they are.' John Brown himself often had one over the eight. Arthur Ponsonby told how his father, Sir Henry Ponsonby, the Queen's private secretary, went in search of Brown after the Queen had been waiting for him in her carriage. He found him lying in his bed dead drunk. Sir Henry locked the door, went outside, and without saying anything took Brown's place on the box. 'The Queen knew what it was and knew that he knew,' said Arthur. 'But on this and other occasions she turned a blind eye.'

Victoria always found an excuse for a tipsy servant's 'over-indulgence'. If he was unsteady on his feet through too much drink the Queen said he was 'unwell'. Edith Sitwell related how, when Brown crashed to the ground in a drunken stupor, the Queen tried to cover it up by saying that she had felt a slight earth tremor. What she said about alcoholic 'tremors' at the ghillies' ball is not recorded, but there is little doubt that on that night she thought just about everything was excusable.

'Fritz' Ponsonby described the ball as 'Bacchanalian'. It was held in a specially erected marquee and was attended in the early part of the evening by the Queen and other members of the Royal Family. When Victoria was having dinner about two hours later the servants waiting on her were often under the influence. Drunken footmen would pour wine all over the table and loud crashes could be heard in the kitchen as plates and dishes were dropped. The Queen continued with her meal as if nothing had gone wrong.

A whole bottle of whisky was provided for any guest out stalking and if the guest didn't drink it the keeper did. 'It was quite a common thing for a stalker to come to the castle and drink off a glass of neat whisky before he started,' wrote Ponsonby's son. 'Of course, if he went out stalking no harm was done, but when the weather was impossible and the mist came down he retired to his house and started the day slightly intoxicated.' After a shoot, the dead stags were laid out in a line by the light of the ghillies' torches. The Queen would inspect the 'kill' and toasts were made, but after Victoria left 'it became an orgy'.

When the Prince of Wales became King Edward VII he took steps to stop such excessive drinking. Stalkers were limited to a flask of whisky instead of a bottle when they went on to the hill for the day. A man who had thirty years' service was dismissed for being drunk when the royal shooting party was ready to have lunch.

I left Willie Blair's house and its ghosts and headed back up the 'whisky road' where the first distillery had been built, then on past Catanellan and Tornauran, with its memories of the McDonald family. When I cleared the woods I found myself at the field I had crossed coming down from Tom Builteach. Now I was seeing Lena Cruickshank's map from ground level – the Chapel Park, Lochnagar Lodge ('The Bungalow'), the old schoolhouse, Lochnagar distillery, and away in the distance, Prince Albert's pyramid cairn on Craig Luragain.

I looked back to Tom Builteach, but it nursed its secrets. The only thing I had discovered about it was that two ancient stone age cists, or graves, were found 'near the top of the eminence called the Tom of the Boltchach, upon the farm of the Lochnagar Distillery'. The cists were about thirty-three inches long by about twenty wide, constructed of rough flagstones. I wondered again who had built the cairn, and why, and if there had been a celebration there, with Willie Blair playing his fiddle and sharing a bottle with the ghillies. I never found out. I passed the distillery and went on to Easter Balmoral and the South Deeside road. The steep slope down to it was shown on Lena's map. It was, appropriately, called The Still Brae.

9

Civil bonnets

An old coaching inn stands by the roadside at Inver, two miles west of Crathie on the north Deeside road. It was built on the edge of a wilderness of moor and mountain stretching out through Aberarder to Gairnside and Tomintoul and west to the far reaches of the Dee. To the south is the vast sprawl of the Garmaddie Woods, where Queen Victoria often walked when staying at Balmoral.

I remember a picture that once hung on the wall of the inn. It was by Deeside's 'forgotten photographer', Robert Milne (see chapter 12), and it

9.1 *The Inver Hotel*

showed life as it was in the old days. A coach and four stood outside, creaking under the weight of its passengers. There were ten travellers on top, bearded and bowler-hatted, packed like sardines, sitting on the edge of disaster. Inside, there were more passengers and up in front sat the coachman, resplendent in top hat and high-buttoned tunic. A group of people had gathered to see the coach set off on its journey to Braemar and a man in a dog-cart had turned his head to watch the coach go on its way.

When you compare the building shown in the picture with the present-day inn it seems as if nothing has changed. The most noticeable difference is in the sign on the wall – 'Invercauld Arms'. Now it says 'Inver Hotel'. The changing of the name must have had something to do with the fact that there was an Invercauld Arms Hotel in Braemar, but it is sad to think that an old coaching inn should end up simply as a 'hotel'.

The first time I saw the picture I wondered if the top-hatted coachman was old John Irvine, who was the first man to run a coach on Deeside. The Aberdeen historian, Joseph Robertson, described him as 'the beau ideal of a coach-guard'. There was not, he wrote, a single tree, house, hill, ale-house, inn, man or child on the whole wayside that Irvine didn't know. He was humorous, frequently garrulous, but when he was in a bad humour he could be 'coarse and unaccommodating'. His most serious crime was that he sometimes harnessed horses that were unfit to drag the coach.

Robertson mentioned John Irvine in an article in the *Aberdeen Magazine*, written 'in the inn at Banchory Ternan, where we have whiffed our cigar these several days past'. The article deplored the fact that Deeside had been 'desolated by Cockneys and other horrible reptiles'. They had descended on the valley like a swarm of locusts, said Robertson – 'the inns sit crammed with them to the very chimney tops, the turnpikes teem with their infernal post chaises, the woods are filled with their picnics and the birds screamed to death by their squalling.'

The year was 1831 – and tourism had arrived on Deeside. Robertson was concerned at the invasion of visitors from the south, but, having taken a swipe at 'the scum of Brummagen and Sheffield, the miserable outcasts of Worthing, and the rejected of Margate', he then proceeded to extol the attractions which Deeside had to offer. Sipping his whisky punch, puffing his fat cigar, he decided: 'We may as well commence with a eulogy on the inns.' The eulogy turned out to be more like a nineteenth-century *Which* report on the inns and ale-houses of Deeside and their hosts. Special attention was given to food and drink – and girls.

Robertson, who was to become a distinguished writer and historian – the greatest of all Aberdeen's historians, it was said – had an eye for a pretty girl in his younger days. The starting point for his tour was an inn at Park, thirteen miles from Aberdeen, which provided excellent breakfasts, dinners and suppers. Robertson was waited on by 'one of the prettiest girls on Deeside'. There were two inns at Banchory, the New Inn – which he had never visited because he hated new inns – and Torrie's Inn, where he was staying. His comments on Torrie's were restrained, but one thing he wanted to see 'mended' was 'the landlord's surly face when draggd out of bed by belated travellers'.

Eight miles on at Kincardine O'Neil it was a different story. Here there was an inn which made them smack their lips – 'glorious breakfasts, splendid dinners, magnificent suppers – and pretty chambermaids'. Not only that, there was an obliging, bustling, buxom hostess, who dished out drams from her own private bottle. They 'drunk many tumblers' in this hostelry before staggering off to the 'soft, clean well-aired beds' prepared by the chambermaids. Robertson said his 'thank you' in verse.

> Of all the hostelries so fair,
> Built for the travellers dwelling,
> On Deeside far beyond compare
> Kincardine is excelling.

Visitors were still smacking their lips at this Kincardine inn – the Gordon Arms – almost to the end of the twentieth century (I still remember sitting at a roaring fire there many years ago scoffing a plate of hot stovies), but in 1998 it was severely damaged by fire and closed down. It opened again in time to see out the century and welcome in a non-stovie millennium.

Robertson continued west to a 'nice, quiet retired hostelry at Charleston of Aboyne'. He said he could safely recommend it, but didn't actually name it, and from there he moved diffidently on to Ballater, expecting the worst. He remembered that on an earlier visit to Ballater he had to wait two hours and twenty-three minutes for breakfast and he recalled begging for a couple of chairs and a hearth-rug to sleep on.

But Ballater was changing. When Robertson returned to it it had become a 'gay, populous place' with an elegant hotel where breakfast was 'set down almost before the bell-rope has ceased to swing'. There were also girls! He could sit there in the evening with a jug of punch at his elbow and 'write a pair of sonnets or an irregular ode or two to some one or other of the pretty girls sauntering – sweet little dears that they are! – on the other side of the river'.

'There are other sundry smaller and more retired places of entertainment between Ballater and Braemar,' he wrote, 'of which, as they scarcely approach the dignity of an inn, it does not become us here to speak.' He did, however, mention 'our other host at Tennabich', although he couldn't remember the man's name. This was Tynabaich, a former farm west of Crathie, now a house.

It was not uncommon at one time for farms to act as drinking howffs for passing travellers. The Monaltrie Arms at Ballater also got a pat on the back. He said it offered 'a dinner as good as your appetite', and the appetite of this nineteenth century Egon Ronay was always good. At Braemar there were two inns, the Farquharson Arms (the Invercauld) and the Fife Arms, which tempted him with 'haunches of venison, venison pasties, *usquebaugh* of the true peat-reek flavour, honey, heather honey, jellies, marmalades, hill mutton, trout fresh from the Dee, and all the delicacies of the season'. The man that fared ill at Braemar, he said, had only himself to blame.

Two innkeepers were given top ratings, one at Coilacreich, near Ballater, the other at the Inver. 'The princely palace of Coilecreich', as Robertson described it, is run today by Willie Meston, secretary of the Braemar Royal Highland Society. His nineteenth-century predecessor seems to have plied Robertson with plenty of *usquebaugh* – enough, at any rate, to take his mind off girls, for he rambled on at length about the inn-keeper's physique. It sounded as if he was talking about a Highland bull, not a man: 'broad shoulders, well-turned haunches, and strong-knit leg.' Willie Meston would have passed the test on all three counts, for he is an imposing figure in the kilt, having nothing in common with the 'bent and bowed, sallow, hollow-eyed, blue-face creatures' despised by Robertson.

Coilacriech is a down-to-earth hostelry that is a world away from the plush hotels and guest houses that have sprung up on Deeside. It still retains something of the character of an old coaching inn, as does the Inver, where two famous coaches, the *Royal Highlander* and the *Earl of Aboyne*, once stopped to pick up passengers going over the Devil's Elbow to Perth. The landlord at the Inver was a 'venerable patriach' called James Leys, who was more commonly known by the name of 'Civil Bonnets'. He was said to always have a 'whisky bottle and bow' ready for visitors. Deacon Alexander Robb, an Aberdeen tailor who was known to scribble out a piece of doggerel at the drop of a hat – or bonnet – used the nickname in a verse about a coach which took him to 'our lov'd Queen's retreat':

> Now ceased the drivers, or the pipes their din,
> Till we arriv'd at Civil Bonnet's inn.

How Leys got the nickname is a bit of a mystery. It is obvious that he was a well-known and popular landlord, a civil man, a 'noble host', said Robertson, but where bonnets came into it is anybody's guess. It becomes more confusing when you remember that the word 'bonnet' has an unhappy connotation at Inver, for it was near here at Ballochlaggan that eighteen bonnet lairds were hung from the rafters of a 'gyrt barn' for upsetting the laird; bonnet lairds were small landlords who farmed their own land.

The name Leys was well known on Upper Deeside in the nineteenth century. Tombstones in Crathie kirkyard tell of Leys who lived and died in the parish. In one corner here are eight memorials to members of the Leys family. Many of them, like Alexander Leys from Sliach, a farm (now deserted) on Glen Gairn, were born at the Crofts of Aberarder. The ruins of this old settlement lie on a hill overlooking the Fclagie Burn, which wanders lazily east to join the Fearder.

It was there that a young girl called Margaret Leys spent her early years. Her father, Charles Leys, had a 'smiddy' and a holding at the Crofts. He could never have imagined that one day his daughter would provide him with a grandson whose name would be known from one end of the country to the other. He would become a 'friend more than servant' to Queen Victoria, books would be written about him, films would be made, and long after his death people would argue over his relationship with the Queen. They called him John Brown after his father.

The elder John Brown was known as 'Jamie', perhaps because many Leys of different generations had the same first name, and Jamie's wife, Margaret, was often called 'Mrs Jamie'. They had eleven children, nine sons and two daughters, but a typhoid epidemic that swept through Crathie in the winter of 1849 claimed three of their children within a month – Francis, aged ten, Margaret, fourteen, and Charles, who was seventeen. John was their second child.

In September, 1998, I wrote an article in *Leopard Magazine* on Margaret Leys titled 'The Other Mrs Brown'. A few weeks later I received a letter from a Mrs Dorathy Leys, who lived in Kelowna, British Columbia, in Canada, and had been sent a copy of the magazine. Her husband, Douglas Leys, had died in October 1964, and her search for his forebears began when her four children started asking if she knew anything about their father's family. 'I didn't,' she told me.

So for ten years Dorathy worked to put together a geneaology of the Deeside Leys. The family tree that she drew up showed that her husband, Douglas, had a link with the Leys of Aberarder. John Brown's mother, Margaret Leys, was his fourth cousin. At the top of the Leys family tree were two brothers – Charlie, the blacksmith (Margaret Leys' father), who was born in 1770, and James Leys, the innkeeper, born in 1757.

The Leys were prominent in the affairs of Upper Deeside. In 1832, when Crathie church formed a board of health for the parish, a list was drawn up of 'respectable heads of families' who could serve on its committees. The name of James Leys – Auld Jamie – the 'venerable patriarch' as Joseph Robertson had called him, was put forward. He would have been seventy-five at the time. The name of his son Charles, who was first cousin to Margaret Leys, was also put forward. He was thirty-one. Francis Leys, John Brown's uncle, was also an elder of Crathie kirk.

Today, many of the old farms scattered about Aberarder are in ruins, but one farm has survived the years – Ballochlaggan, notorious as the place where the bonnet lairds were hanged. This building was once the home of the Leys. James Leys married Margaret Farquharson, daughter of Colonel John Farquharson, at Ballochlaggan in 1781, and Francis Leys died there in 1884 at the age of eighty-two. He was the last Leys to live at Ballochlaggan.

So the pieces of this genealogical jigsaw began to come together. Dorathy Leys, explaining her complicated family tree, wrote: 'I am putting bits and pieces together to finish it, but these never seem to be at an end.' She discovered that there were still two pieces that might fit into the picture. They came from Donald Grant, a friend of mine, a man who loved Aberarder and spent many happy childhood days there, not far from where John Brown's mother had lived. Dorathy had written to him because she learned that his mother was called Leys, but, in fact, there was no close connection with Auld Jamie's side of the family.

Nevertheless, there was one unexpected link between Auld Jamie and Donald Grant's father. More than a century after James Leys had welcomed guests to his pub with 'a whisky bottle and a bow', Donald Grant senior – Donald Kennedy Grant – became mine host at Civil Bonnet's inn, the Inver. It was during his years there that he kept a diary which drew a fascinating picture of life on Upper Deeside in the early years of the last century.

His diary was an old cash notebook into which he wrote what he called 'a short story on the life of Donald Kennedy Grant, born on 25th January 1885'. It told of how he started his working life as a fee'd loon in Glencat, grew up, ran a grocer's shop in Aberdeen, and in 1920 left the city to take over the Inver Inn, or the Inver Crathie Hotel as he called it.

I had four horses, three milk cows, hens, ducks and one hotel lodger, but had the wife, her mother and Aunt Nell and of course wee Donald [his newly born son] within a short time. So my farming and hotel life began. The horse had to be disposed of and two good ones bought. They were very expensive then, a good one over £100, but I made a good buy as I had both for my whole time at Inver.

The hotel trade then was pretty poor as there was only one bus per day which carried passengers to and from Ballater trains. It also carried the mail to Crathie and Braemar and was then delivered by postmen or

9.2 Donald Kennedy Grant

women. The Corndavon postman on his round met the Queen [Victoria] with a shooting party and in the conversation she asked him how long it would take him to cycle from that point. He replied 'Twal meenits full oot.' The Queen thought he was foreign and asked the gamekeeper what he meant, which was twelve minutes as fast as he could go.

Donald was given the contract to drive school pupils to Crathie 'with a brown brought from Bracmar Castle which had belonged to a Russian Princess'. A 'brown' was a brown horse, which may have been taken over during the visit to Balmoral in 1896 of the Emperor Nicholas II and the Empress Alexandra Feodorovna of Russia. 'We managed in summer with one horse,' wrote Donald, 'but in winter required two horses. It was a well-paid job but pretty tough in winter – snow and ice and the storms, then mere mud, worse than snow, sometimes eighteen inches deep.'

The Inver was a popular drinking howff for gamekeepers and Donald Grant came to know most of them, so he had 'lots of stalking and lots of funny experiences in the hills'. He recalled one in the Slugan Glen, on the Invercauld estate. There was a shooting lodge in the glen where 'an Invercauld lady had been sent to have a child to one of the gardeners'. The scandal had long blown over before Donald went shooting there, for he mentioned that the lodge had been 'a ruin for some time'. Slugan is called the Fairy Glen and the ruined lodge is still well known to hill-walkers.

Donald's hunting party consisted of the head stalker, two under-keepers, plus a cart and horse with a man to take the deer home.

> Our journey proved to be a disaster. Firstly, the journey in a cart which had iron rings on the wheels, might have been very suitable to bring home dead deer, but on the rocky road one would have required to have a rubber bottom.
>
> Did not stay long in the cart and our journey proved futile. We saw at least 100 hinds but the stalker said not to fire. We returned without a shot from Slugan but my luck changed on the way home. Saw a hind's head appear about 50 yards in the wood, crept up quietly and shot three nice hinds within one mile of home.

Donald described how he went out for a night's salmon poaching – with a local ghillie!

> This had been going on for years up the hill burn, no fishing rod, just a cycle lamp and a gaff. The first one I gaffed my foot slipped on a wet stone and I went in the water overhead but got my fish. Had a very exciting night, plenty fish and gallons of booze to keep the cold out. It seemed to be an annual event and the party knew where the water bailiffs were.

Donald eventually left the Inver and took over the Grant Arms Hotel in Fochabers, but seven years later moved to the Seafield Arms in Cullen. He sold his Cullen hotel some time after the Second World War and returned to Deeside, where he worked as a ghillie on various estates. He recalled having 'a

9.3 *Auntie Nell's house in Aberarder*

few words' with a chap who stuck his boat in the river and his fly up near the top of a tree. The man wanted to know why others were getting fish and he was getting none. 'Well, sir,' said Donald bluntly, 'ye canna fish.'

So that was Donald Kennedy Grant. 'Wee Donald', now in his seventies, looks back on his Inver days with great nostalgia. His roots lie deep in Aberarder; his mother, Annie, and her sister Helen (Auntie Nell) were both employed at Balmoral Castle in the service of Queen Victoria. They worked alongside many of the Indian servants brought to Balmoral by Victoria, including the famous Munshi Abdul Karim (see chapter 13). Auntie Nell had a cottage at Middleton of Aberarder and young Donald spent all his school holidays there. It was, he said, the best days of his life.

Old tracks reach out from Aberarder, one going west by Felagie and Keiloch to the Invercauld bridges, another striking north by Balnoe and Ratlich

(James Leys' daughter Barbara was married at the farm of Ratlich), and a 'middle road' which once took you through the Middleton clachan to Balloch, Am Bealach, a pass leading to the Bealach Dearg and over the hills to Loch Builg and Inchrory.

When G. M. Fraser was writing *The Old Deeside Road*, published in 1920, he visited Aberarder and saw 'scarcely a soul except at a few huts at

9.4 *Jean Cattanach outside her cottage at Keiloch*

Middleton'. One could hardly believe, he added, that this isolated glen was at one time well populated; in the second half of the twentieth century it got worse. Ruins at Balloch, ruins at Balnoe, ruins at Felagie, ruins at Knockan, and at Middleton, nothing – life had seeped out of Aberarder like a leaking tap.

But Donald Grant still has his memories. I remember him showing me a photo album which turned back the years. There was a photograph of his father, Donald Kennedy Grant, with a huge white collar and a sprig of heather in his buttonhole, and another of his grandfather, the grandly named Francis Adolphus Grant, with a long grey beard, a keeper's hat on his head, a jacket fastened only by the top button and a gun on his arm. Francis lived in the Fungle at Aboyne and was gamekeeper to Sir William Cunliffe-Brooks, the eccentric laird of Glentanar; he named one of his sons William Cunliffe Grant. There were also pictures of the Munshi and Rondy, the Queen's chef, and a snap of Auntie Nell's house, with a caption underneath it saying that the laird of Invercauld had razed it to the ground.

Donald talked about other houses that had vanished, among them Bella Catnoch's house, next to Auntie Nellie's cottage; the gable-end of Lizzie MacHardy's house; the shell of Maggie Lamont's house. The only one that had survived was Jean Cattanach's house, which had been turned into a Girl Guides' hut. I have never forgotten what Jean said to visitors who wanted to go to the toilet. 'Go out the door,' she said, 'cross the moss, and turn your arse to Craig Leek.' An old cottage at Knockan has been beautifully restored and extended and when I was there work was beginning on adapting the old kirk for housing. Did that mean that life would come back to Aberarder in the new millennium? It seemed unlikely.

In the middle of all this decay and despair, the ghost of the 'venerable patriach' hovers over the Inver Inn. I went back there to find out who had taken on the mantle of Civil Bonnets. The inn (I still call it an inn) is now run by the Mathieson family; Andrew Mathieson used to be a policeman in Strathclyde and came north with his son Fraser to take over the Inver. Fraser and his wife Seonaid are now mine hosts – the Civil Bonnets of the new millennium.

10

Who wears the trousers?

When Donald Kennedy Grant was host at the Inver Inn in the 1920s, he often showed his customers a statuette of another man called Grant – John Grant, once head forester to Prince Albert and Queen Victoria – 'an excellent man', according to the Queen, 'most trustworthy, of singular shrewd-ness and discretion'. The statuette was a mould – and the completed silver figure cast from it can still be seen in the summer exhibition in the ballroom at Balmoral Castle.

The statuette is about twenty inches high. When the silver figures in the ballroom were made the sculptors were allowed to keep the plaster casts and the one of John Grant eventually landed up in his namesake's inn at Inver. Local folk who saw it perched on the bar instantly recognised it, for the sculpted figure wore a pair of trousers, not the kilt. John Grant was the only member of the Queen's staff allowed to wear trousers instead of traditional dress, although Victoria sometimes relaxed the rules for her guests. When the artist Edwin Landseer was invited to Balmoral, the Queen's private secretary, Sir Charles Phipps, wrote to tell him that 'the usual evening costume is the kilt, worn by everybody who claims to wear one, but at anyrate we are not par-ticular in these mountainous districts, and many of Her Majesty's guests appear in Trousers'.

In the days when Aberdeen's pioneer photographer George Washington Wilson was becoming known, there were many photographs of Victoria's ghillies and keepers. In group pictures, John Grant always stood out from the rest – he was the only one wearing trousers. Even in family pictures he remained kiltless. In one photograph taken at the door of Rhebreck, his house in the grounds of Balmoral, he was seen with his wife, his daughter Victoria, and his six sons, John, Alex, James, Arthur, Albert and Andrew. The boys all wore the kilt, but their father wore trousers. Why Grant rejected the kilt is something of a mystery, and even more puzzling is the fact that the Queen allowed it. It may be that the keeper stuck to his guns – and his trousers – and got away with it; Victoria often gave way to people who stood up to her.

There is a well-known photograph of the Queen sitting side-saddle on her pony 'Fyvie', with a kilted John Brown holding the reins. John Grant is on the

10.1 *The statuette of John Grant*

right of the picture, carrying Victoria's cape over his arm. As usual, he is wearing trousers. When a new print was made at a later stage the Queen and Brown were seen on their own – Grant had mysteriously vanished. No one seems to know why the picture was doctored in this way. It may have been because of the controversy over Brown's relationship with the Queen. On the other hand, it may have had something to do with Grant's breeks.

Prince Albert wore the kilt, but it was said that his appearance left a lot to be desired. In her book, *Victoria, Queen and Ruler* (1903), Emily Crawford wrote: 'The want of whipcord in his thews (muscles) proclaim that he is no

Highlander.' She believed that the kilt was not becoming to 'gentlemen of German physique'. It needed 'the feline cleanness of build and muscularity of the mountain Celt for the bare knees and legs to look well'. Perhaps Grant looked at his royal master's knees and decided not to expose his own to public gaze.

John Brown was Queen Victoria's 'beloved friend', but John Grant, her 'most trustworthy' keeper, ranked high in her favour. He was the indispensable retainer, the wise old head, who served for twenty years as keeper to Sir Robert Gordon before Balmoral was sold to the Queen. He held the post for nearly thirty years.

His name featured prominently in Victoria's journal. It was Grant who called for three cheers for the Duke of Atholl when they road through Bynack on their way home from Atholl. It was Grant who took her to the obelisk being erected in memory of Prince Albert. 'I thought you would like to be here today,' he said, 'on His birthday.' It was Grant who made a little speech when they went to her 'Widow's House' at Glass-allt on Loch Muick, hoping that 'our Royal Mistress, our good Queen, should live long'. This was what Victoria wrote in her journal:

> We dined about half-past eight in the small dining room. This over, after waiting for a little while in my sitting-room, Brown came to say all the servants were ready for the house-warming, and at twenty minutes to ten we went into the little dining-room, which had been cleared, and where all the servants were assembled, viz., my second dresser, C. Wilmore, Brown, Grant, Ross (who played), Hollis (the cook), Lady Churchill's maid, Maxted, C. and A. Thomson, Blake (the footman who only comes to do duty outside at night). We made nineteen altogether. Five animated reels were danced, in which all (but myself) joined. After the first reel 'whisky-toddy' was brought round for everyone, and Brown begged I would drink to the 'fire-kindling'. Then Grant made a little speech, with an allusion to the wild place we were in, and concluding with a wish 'that our Royal Mistress, our good Queen', should 'live long'. This was followed by cheers given out by Ross in regular Highland style, and all drank my health. The merry pretty little ball ended at a quarter past eleven. The men, however, went on singing in the steward's room, and all were very happy.

Grant was a dour, unsmiling man, but he could speak out when necessary, had a pawkish humour that pleased Prince Albert, and knew how to flatter his royal mistress. He once told the Queen – when she was forty-six – 'Ye can spin as well as any auld woman in the country.' This despite the fact that an old peasant woman picked up a scrap of knitting that the Queen had done and said curtly that she pitied the 'gude man' if he got no better made stockings than that. Grant was sixteen years older than Brown and there was little love lost between them. The entries in Victoria's journal give the impression that they had a good working relationship – here were Grant and Brown 'on the box again'; Grant and Brown waiting on the Queen at dinner; Grant and Brown fooling the public about the mysterious guest at a Fettercairn hotel:

> A traveller had arrived at night, and wanted to come up into the dining room, which is the 'commercial travellers' room', and they had difficulty in telling him he could not stop there. He joined Grant and Brown at their tea, and on asking, 'What's the matter here?' Grant answered, 'It's a wedding party from Aberdeen.' At the Temperance Hotel they were very anxious to know whom they had got. All, except General Grey, breakfasted a little before nine. Brown acted as my servant, brushing my skirt and boots, and taking any message, and Grant as Albert's valet.

At Kingussie, where they were still travelling incognito, Grant and Brown kept a 'chattering crowd' off the royal carriages. Here again, the two keepers put on a double act to fool the natives. 'Grant and Brown kept them off the carriages,' wrote the Queen, 'and gave them evasive answers, directing them to the wrong carriage, which was most amusing. One old gentleman, with a high wide-awake, was especially inquisitive.' (A wide-awake was a felt hat with a broad brim.)

The Queen thought Grant and Brown were perfect, but, privately, there was an intense jealousy between them. It was a question of who *really* 'wore the trousers' at Balmoral. Brown, as the Queen's Highland servant, thought he had authority over all the Highland servants, including John Grant, but Grant refused to take orders from him. There were frequent minor squabbles, such as a dispute between the two men over fishing rights to a particular stretch of the Dee. Grant was Prince Albert's head ghillie and the feud came to Victoria's attention when Prince Albert refused to shake hands with Brown. The Queen gave an order that the quarrel be patched up immediately.

If Grant's standing with the Queen was high, it may have had something to do with his wife's friendship with Queen Victoria. Their daughter was named Victoria, after the Queen. The Queen was wary of literary types and high-sounding intellectuals; she was annoyed when Arthur Helps, who edited her journal, urged her to put her syntax in order. Sir Henry Ponsonby, her private secretary, called him 'Lord Help Us'. After the success of *Leaves*, she was invited to a 'pink tea' held by Lady Augusta Stanley. She found herself ill at ease in the presence of authors such as Carlyle and Browning; Carlyle had just published one of the longest poems in the English language and the Queen was heard to ask innocently, 'Are you writing anything?'

Victoria, fearful of repeating such social blunders, turned to lesser mortals for company, dismissing Carlyle as 'a strange-looking eccentric old Scotchman, who holds forth'. Henry Ponsonby said she preferred the company of Mrs Grant, her head-keeper's wife, to that of the wife of George Grote, the historian. 'Mrs Grant speaks of her children and the tea cakes and scones,' he said, 'but Mrs Grote might suddenly ask her whether she approved of female doctors.' At any rate, the 'pink tea' at Lady Stanley's was never repeated.

There was a room in Mrs Grant's house at Rhebreck set aside for the Queen's use. It was there that Victoria entertained her cousin Princess Mary Adelaide and her husband the Prince of Teck when they visited Balmoral. The princess was nicknamed 'Fat Mary' because of her huge appetite. She had a particular fondness for boiled potatoes, which she gobbled up with gluttonous relish on her picnics on the moors. Writing about an outing to Gelder Shiel, she said: 'We took our share in watching the potatoes, which turned out first-rate and were done ample justice to.' On the day that she left Balmoral she had a snack between breakfast and lunch of scones and jellies at Mrs Grant's.

It was to Mrs Grant's house that the Queen went on a June day in 1872 when two children fell into the Monaltrie Burn and were swept into the Dee. One was three years old; his brother Jemmie, ten or eleven. The Monaltrie Burn, which was originally called the Balnault Burn, runs into the Dee near the farm of Balnaut, about a mile and a half west of Crathie.

We heard from the people that the two boys were at Monaltrie Burn, which comes down close to the farmhouse and below Mrs Patterson's shop, passing under a little bridge and running into the Dee. This burn is generally very low and small, but had risen to a great height – the Dee itself being tremendously high – not a stone to be seen . . . The little child fell in while the eldest was fishing; the other jumped in after him, trying to save his little brother; and before anyone could come out to save them (though the screams of Abercrombie's children, who were with them, were heard) they were carried away and swept by the violence of the current into the Dee, and carried along. Too dreadful! It seems, from what I heard coming back, that the poor mother was away from home, having gone to see her own mother who was dying, and that she purposely kept this eldest boy back to watch the little one. We saw people on the banks and rocks with stick searching; among them was the poor father – sad and piteous sight – crying and looking so anxiously for his poor child's body.

The drowned children came from a cottage at the foot of Craig Nordie, a rocky little hill north-east of the Inver – 'a lovely position', wrote the Queen. After the youngest boy's body had been recovered, Victoria went to the cottage with Brown.

> We went in, and on a table in the kitchen covered with a sheet which they lifted up, lay the poor sweet innocent 'bairnie', only three years old, a fine plump child and looking just as though it slept, with quite a pink colour, and very little scratched, in its last clothes – with his little hands joined.

The Queen went back to the river and sat on the bank to watch the search for the missing boy's body. Grant and Brown were with her. 'When they came to that very deep pool, where twenty-three years ago a man was nearly drowned when they were leistering* for salmon, they held a piece of red cloth on a pole over the water, which enabled them to see down to the bottom. But all in vain.' That evening, a telegram arrived saying that the oldest boy's body had been found on an island opposite Pannanich, below Ballater. Two days later, the funeral was held. 'The poor father walked in front of one of the coffins, both covered with white, and so small,' Victoria wrote. 'It was a very sad sight.'

In May 1879, Queen Victoria celebrated her sixtieth birthday. In November of that year John Grant died at Rhebreck at the age of sixty-nine. When he was ill the Queen visited him almost every day. As she sat by his bedside, perhaps she was thinking of the time she took him to London. 'It was quite a pleasure', she noted, 'to see his honest weather beaten face again, as quiet, demure and plain spoken as usual, in spite of all the novelties around him.' The Queen attended the funeral service of her head forester, held in his house, and arranged for a wall memorial stone to be erected in Crathie kirkyard. He was, it says: 'for 26 years the faithful head forester to the Prince Consort and Queen Victoria.' The death of his wife Elizabeth in 1887 is also recorded. 'Much beloved by Queen Victoria and all the Royal Family,' says the inscription.

But Grant wasn't buried at Crathie, where so many members of the royal staff lie under tombstones erected by the Queen. He belonged to Braemar and

---

* This incident took place in September 1850. The Queen was watching them leistering (spearing salmon) on the Dee when two of them got into trouble. 'We had a great fright,' wrote Victoria. 'In one place there was a very deep pool into which the two men foolishly went, and one could not swim; we suddenly saw them sink, and in one moment they seemed drowning. There was a cry for help and a general rush, including Albert, towards the spot, which frightened me. Dr Robertson swam in and pulled the man out, but it was a horrid moment.'

it was to there that his remains were taken. He was buried in the ancient kirkyard of St Andrew's on the outskirts of the village, where another famous Grant – Peter Grant, the oldest Jacobite rebel – was laid to rest in 1824. Peter, better known as Dubrach from his farm in Glen Dee, was 110 years old when he died. He was an unrepentant rebel, declaring that if he had youth on his side he would 'fecht Culloden ower again'. The graves of John Grant and his parents are side by side. His father, Alexander Grant, a farmer at Easter Balmoral, died in 1846, aged seventy-five, and his mother, Ann McIntosh, died in 1869 aged eighty-seven. The head forester's own stone gives the name of his house as Rebrake.

Grant headstones dominate the St Andrew's kirkyard (there are twenty-nine Grant graves there), but one member of the clan married into a family that seemed eager to claim the longest tenure. Barbara Grant, who died in 1856, was married to John Gruer from Inverey. His headstone is filled with the names of Gruers, dating from 1856 to as late as 1951. No fewer than six Gruer gravestones are lined up on the south side of the kirkyard. The inscription on one of them tells us that the Gruers 'beneath this stone and in two adjoining graves sleep with their forbears'. Also on the headstones are the lines

> Four hundred years have now wheeled round,
> With half a century more,
> Since this has been the burying ground
> Belonging to the Gruers.

Gruer, Gruar, Grewar: the name is spelt in different ways, but to hundreds of walkers and climbers who went into the Deeside hills in the years before the war there was only one Gruer – the legendary Maggie Gruer, who took them into her cottage in Inverey and gave them tea and scones and a 'wee drap Glenlivet'. They were charged a shilling for bed and breakfast and a sixpence if they were hard up. Maggie kept the money in an enamel bucket.

'Hae ye pit yer name in my book?' she would ask. Among those who did put their names in the book were the poet Charles Murray; Henry Alexander, later Sir Henry, Lord Provost of Aberdeen, who wrote *The Cairngorms*; the playwright Robert Kemp; and the author Eric Linklater. Maggie's father, Donald Gruer, worked the croft behind Thistle Cottage and Mrs Gruer often gave a bed to passing hill-walkers, setting the pattern her daughter followed for so many years.

Thistle Cottage was an unlikely guest-house – a modest building with a room on each side of the front door, a small room at the back and two rooms and a 'closet' upstairs. But there was never a 'Full Up' sign on the window, for the byre at the rear of the house had a good supply of clean straw if you were prepared to share it with Maggie's cow. Maggie herself slept in the box-bed in the living room, which was usually heavy with peat smoke. The guests gathered round the fire, where pots and pans burbled on the swey, and Maggie dealt up brown eggs, buttered oatcakes and scones. There was no other hostess on Deeside like her – and there was an ode to Maggie which said it all:

> When ye'd plytered through the
> Lairig and ye looked an unco sicht
> Or ye'd peched and tyauved and
> Trachled owre Macdhui's steeny hicht'
> And ye felt jist fair forfochen and
> Ye kent nae whaur to camp,
> Oh, a bed at Maggie Gruer's was
> Sae welcome on the tramp.

There is nothing on the inscription over her grave in St Andrew's cemetery to show that the Margaret Gruer buried there was Maggie Gruer, the hill-walkers' friend, but her epitaph had been written a long time before in her visitors' book at Thistle Cottage. 'Scones?' it read. 'In loving memory!'

The kirkyard where John Grant is buried is shrouded in Victorian gloom, filled with the gravestones of Grants and Lamonts and Gruers and McDonalds. 'Pray for their souls,' says the faded lettering on the stones. 'Of your charity pray for the repose of their souls.' Rising in the centre of the graveyard is a small unlovely stone structure like an imitation castle: it is the mausoleum of Farquharsons of Invercauld, erected on the site of the early St Andrew's church. A short distance to the east is Braemar Castle, which some experts dismiss as a sham castle because of its English-style crenellations and battlemented upper works. It dates from 1628 and was built by the 18th Earl of Mar. Nearly four centuries later it belongs to the Farquharsons of Invercauld.

Victoriana still reigns in the Queen's Country. They still talk about the Queen and John Brown, her personal attendant, arguing over how *personal* their relationship really was. A film called *Mrs Brown*, with Judi Dench as Victoria and Billy Connolly as Brown, gave fresh impetus to the argument in the late 1990s, but if John Brown's ghost still hovers over the Braes o' Mar, his rival, John Grant, the Queen's 'most trustworthy' head forester, is long forgotten.

In 1902, the year after Queen Victoria died, Patricia Lindsay wrote about the memorials erected in Crathie churchyard and described John Grant's memorial tablet as one of the warmest tributes paid by the Queen to Balmoral staff buried in the kirkyard. This is what Mrs Lindsay said about him:

10.2 *The statue of John Brown in the grounds of Balmoral*

He was in many respects a typical Highlander both in appearance and character, tall and dark, with a striking strongly marked face, the expression when at rest somewhat 'dour' and hard, but lit up now and then by flashes of pawky humour. Grant was deeply attached to his royal mistress and consequently inclined himself to be jealous when, as he thought, others were preferred before him. This is the penalty often paid by the bestower and receiver of a strong and exclusive devotion, but none knew better than the Queen that it was a leal-hearted, faithful servant to whom, though dead, she yet testifies on the wall of Crathie churchyard.

Now, a century later, no one remembers the Man Who Wore Trousers. The only link with those far-off days is the silver figure of him in the ballroom of Balmoral Castle, and the statuette which Donald Kennedy Grant once displayed in the Inver Inn.

11

An attack of 'jumpers'

Aberdeen's pioneering photographer, George Washington Wilson, decided in 1859 to set off on a photographic tour of the Dee valley – to the 'linns and corries of our Deeside Highlands'. This was a forerunner of many tours into some of the remotest and wildest corners of Scotland, using inadequate maps (and sending corrections to the map-makers), living rough and coping with a mass of equipment; a cumbersome camera, a tent, baskets of chemicals, plate boxes and 'a Vasculum or two'.

George Walker, an Aberdeen bookseller, accompanied him on his expeditions. The difficulties and trials they experienced on their trips were 'almost inconceivable'. In those early days there were no railway lines linking remote areas in the Highlands, and districts with comfortable hotels were practically inaccessible. In many of the out-of-the-way places they had to put up in hovels where cattle drovers were the only customers.

'The beds were extremely suspicious,' wrote Walker, 'and in order to protect ourselves from the attacks of "jumpers" we had not only to sponge ourselves, but to sprinkle the very beds with cheap but extremely powerful whisky. We had to depend for our very existence on dried venison, which required a hatchet to chop it up and steam grinders to masticate it. We were treated to savoury sausages, very highly spiced, which in our tours of discovery were found to consist of "braxie mutton" – sheep found dead on the hills!'

For the most part, doctors were well out of reach, but local inhabitants told them what medicine to take if they were sick – one glass of whisky for discomfort, two glasses for an ailment, and three glasses for serious illness! If that didn't effect a cure, they said, the case was hopeless and the patient was not worth preserving.

Walker likened their travels to 'the experiences of Dr Johnson and his henchman Boswell'. He was Wilson's Boswell, sending back weekly reports to the *Aberdeen Herald*, taking notes for a seventeen-page journal (now in Aberdeen Public Library), and gathering material for a book he was to write called *Aberdeen Awa'*. It all added up to a fascinating account of life on Deeside a century and a half ago – and a glimpse of the problems faced by the city's pioneer photographer in his early days with a camera.

THE LINN OF DEE. 2. GWW.

11.1 *The Linn of Dee (George Washington Wilson)*

Wilson had already taken landscapes for Queen Victoria in 1857 and 1858, including some on Deeside, but the idea of a foray into the little-known 'linns and corries' of the area had come from Walker. The bookseller was one of Wilson's closest friends and often travelled with him on his photographic outings. 'He had the eye of an artist', he wrote, 'and had my preference for wild natural scenery. I never cared for showplaces he was obliged to photograph to supply the demand and I never accompanied him to these, but to any out-of-the-way place he always preferred my company to anyone else, and we revelled in wild glens, mountains and cataracts.'

11.2 *Free church and Burnett Arms Hotel, Banchory*
(George Washington Wilson)

Later, when Wilson set up a network of retail agencies, Walker was in at the birth of what was to become a boom industry. He placed a large order for a 'tolerable view' of the Old Mill at Cults and sold the photographs at 2s. each. He soon became the major retailer of Wilson's photographs in Aberdeen.

The rain fell in torrents on the day they were due to leave Aberdeen. Hail mingled with the rain, thunder rumbled and roared in the darkened skies – 'Heaven's artillery rattling among the chimney tops,' was how Walker described it – and in the country people were astonished to see 'blin' drift'. It helped to speed their departure from the city. Their cases and camera equipment were stowed away in the luggage van of the train and they settled down comfortably in their 'commodious carriages'.

The line to Banchory was opened in September 1853, and extended to Aboyne in 1859, the year they set out on their photographic tour. As their train rumbled out of Aberdeen station, whistling a raucous farewell to the city, they must have seen themselves at the dawn of a new era in travel. They could never have imagined what 'progress' would do in the next century and a half, leaving the Deeside line an empty track, but Walker was looking back, not forward. Twenty years had passed since his last visit to Braemar and he was anxious to see what changes had taken place.

So away went the intrepid travellers, their train puffing past Dr Morison's Bridge (the 'Shakkin' Briggie', once a link across the Dee, now long since demolished) and on past Culter 'with its bonnie woods and its busy mills' and Drum with 'its old romantic keep', then on to Banchory Station, which they saw as 'almost, if not altogether, unique in beauty as a railway terminus'.

Banchory was becoming a commuter town even in 1859. This 'nice little village', said Walker, was 'fast developing itself as a permanent home for men who transact their business in Aberdeen'. A picture by Wilson of the old Free Church and the Burnett Arms Hotel in Banchory shows little sign of a commuter rush in the nice little village. A little girl stands in the middle of the deserted High Street watching the proceedings. I have often wondered if she ever grew up to discover that the funny man with the camera was the famous photographer George Washington Wilson.

From Banchory they went on to Aboyne by coach, complaining that the driver, who had once driven the famous *Defiance*, now held the reigns of an inferior vehicle. Still, they were impressed by the changes that had taken place in what had been 'a dull half-way house with an indifferent inn'. Now it had become a lodging-house village as well as a commuter village. There were 'classical' waiters in lace neckties and sportsmen with Turkish caps: 'Handsome carriages are arriving and departing and fashion rules the day alike in equipages, silk gowns and knickerbockers.'

At Ballater, they discovered that there was a scarcity of visitors that year. Although new lodging places were being opened up by the coming of the railway, Walker thought that the scarcity would continue 'until the people of Ballater learn to provide lodgings on more moderate terms, and cease to fleece visitors on all the necessaries and comforts of life'.

Next morning, they prepared to make 'an ascent of the Poulach hill, overlooking the village'. The route they took seems to have been the old public path from Ballater to Mount Keen, crossing the Pollagach Burn as it runs down to join the Dee at Ballaterach. They carried their photographic gear, a good supply of water, and a tent, which they pitched 'at a respectful distance from the ant hills'. The sun lurked behind the clouds, refusing to come out, and they waited and waited. They watched the coach from Aberdeen arrive and leave for Braemar without them. Finally, they gave up, clambering downhill to get a meal before leaving for Balmoral in a dog-cart.

Now they were deep in the Queen's Country. They were captivated by the sight of Abergeldie Castle, its turret gleaming over the trees on the opposite bank of the Dee. 'It looked so temptingly lovely in the calm summer evening,' wrote Walker, 'that, stopping the dog-cart, we encamped on the level green and took a picture of it with the long shadows of its tall poplars across the white walls, its primitive rope-basket bridge for an avenue.'

The bridge consisted of a rope suspended from posts on either side of the river, with passengers carried in a cradle or basket hanging from it. Once into the cradle the passenger was carried halfway across without any effort on his part and from there had to lever himself up on to the far bank by pulling on the rope with his hands. Not surprisingly, there were a number of accidents. A gauger chasing whisky smugglers across the river was drowned when the rope broke and pitched him into the water.

Then there was the tragedy of two young lovers – Peter Frankie, a game-keeper at Altnaguibhsaich, and his bride Barbara Brown – who were drowned on their wedding day. Barbara was a beautiful and popular girl and there were rumours that a disappointed suitor was responsible for the accident. In 1885 a suspension footbridge was erected by Queen Victoria, but today it is a rusty ruin, pushed into disuse by the motor car.

Further on, Wilson and his companion passed 'a collection of rude stone hovels which seem, as they stand in all conceivable positions, to have rolled down the hillside with the brawling burn beside them, or had fallen from the clouds without any arrangement at all'. I remember coming on the same scene – and feeling the same sense of surprise – when I was searching for the remains of old settlements for my book, *Land of the Lost*. This was the Micras, whose crumbling walls formed strange shapes and patterns on the slopes above the North Deeside road.

The writer John Grant Michie was born at the Micras in 1830 and gave a vivid description of a typical township there in his book *Deeside Tales*: 'A clachan built of turf or divot, or stone and clay at the best, with nothing but timber lums and pitiful small windows.' There was a dung-heap a few feet from the door, a pig-stye at the back, an ash-pit and hens roosting inside the houses. Michie's book would have been well known by the late 1850s and it is surprising that the Aberdeen bookseller didn't know about the Micras.

It was from there that they got their first glimpse of Balmoral across the river – Walker called it the palace, which was what the locals called it in its early days.

> Cairns of stone, like huge extinguishers, erected by the tenantry to commemorate the marriage of the Princess Royal crowned several of the elevations; flags waved from two or three points in honour of the Duchess of Kent's birthday. White rustic chimneys, gleaming amid foliage and neat cottages, half nestling in the woods, showed the habitations of keepers, *et hoc genus omne*, and showed that we were approaching the Palace. As we rounded the ridge on which Crathie kirk stands the quarters rung out bold and clear, a deep-toned bell sounded the hour, and a massive white granite tower rising over a number of roofs announced Balmoral.

They passed the bridge to Balmoral – 'a fine iron bridge, erected by Prince Albert at an expense of £5,000' – and came to Crathie Cottage, with its 'smug little garden and artistic gateway', hoping to get lodgings there for the night, but every room was occupied. Crathie Cottage, at the corner of the road to Bush, was known as Chrystals; it was named after an Alexander Chrystal who lived there in 1851. Down on the main road there was a smithy called Crystall's smiddy.

Unable to get a room for the night, they went on to Inver, 'famed of yore as having been kept by "Civil Bonnets"' (see chapter 9), but in the evening they went back to Crathie. They found the approach to Balmoral disappointing:

> An unsightly washing-house with whitewashed walls blackened with soot and smoke, stares you out of countenance and brings down one's idea of the place. Its chimneys mingled with the roofs of stables and servants' houses, also too prominently in view, and in a line beyond the tower and turrets of the Castle rise, giving an idea at first of a long unruly village with a large lock up house.

But the nearer they got to the 'palace' the better it looked: 'a handsome edifice . . . finely dressed beautiful granite . . . all in good taste.'

On their way up Deeside, George Walker was remembering his visit twenty years earlier.

> Then it was less known and less run after than now. Visitors had the most entire freedom and complete range of the hills, forests and glens

at their disposal. We fished in the streams and lochs and to some pur-pose, too, as our baskets frequently showed. The very policies of Invercauld house were not so sacred but that we could traverse them.

Wilson and Walker were shown round Invercauld House, although Walker remained quiet on the identity of their guide, merely saying that it was done 'with a little management'. They inspected the house, admired the crowned stags' heads in the hall, the fine Cairngorm crystals in the museum, and the furniture and paintings. 'The very beer cellar was shown, and we tippled at home-brew, which blazed on the application of a light. After this we were treated to a pibroch on a pair of prize bagpipes in the servants' hall, the screigh of which, blown out by a tempestuous prize Highlander in the large stone-vaulted apartment, rings in our ears to this day.'

Braemar was to be their base and it was there that their real work began. The two men headed west in their dog-cart to the Linn of Dee, with its 'hand-some new stone bridge' opened by Queen Victoria two years before Wilson's foray into Upper Deeside. Here, they were on the edge of the wilderness, the 'vast solitudes', as Walker put it, which had become the hunting ground of deer stalkers; now they were being emptied even more to make way for the deer. Walker wrote:

> Twenty years ago, sheep used to dot all the hills. Now the sheep farms are shut up and the buildings ruinous. In many a glen the rowan tree under which the bairnies sat and played, the grassy hillock and the greener mounds, are the only remains of what was once a home. In a few years more the visitor from Canada or Australia who comes to this country to see his birthplace will find it difficult or impossible to say where the hearthstone stood.

They saw the first signs of depopulation when they went through Inverey, which was originally two hamlets – Meikle Inverey and Little Inverey. 'We drove westwards,' wrote Walker, 'passing Corriemulzie Cottage, perched like a dove's nest under the shelter of the Raven's Crag, and the new bridge to Mar Lodge.' Corriemulzie Cottage, which was later renamed New Mar Lodge to mark it out from the first Mar Lodge, was destroyed by fire in 1895. Queen Victoria danced at Corriemulzie. 'It was a beautiful and most unusual sight,' she wrote. The dance board was entirely surrounded by Highlanders carrying torches. There were seven pipers playing together and three Highlanders danced a reel holding torches in their hands.

Past Corriemulzie, Wilson and Walker came to Glen Ey. 'Conspicuous above the Highland village, which formerly was a collection of rude hovels, stand some neat gamekeepers' lodges of a superior style, while in the centre of the village an old wall of thirty feet in height, with some slits and narrow windows, is all that remains of the Castle of Inverey, the seat of a freebooter, Farquharson.' The ruins of the castle are still there today, but the slits and narrow windows have gone. Inverey stands at the mouth of a glen whose people were evicted in the mid-1800s. 'Skeleton tree and skeleton townships,' I wrote in *Land of the Lost*. 'Never has desolation been more evident than in this forgotten glen.'

Wilson took his camera up Glen Ey to photograph the Colonel's Bed, a rocky shelf where the Black Colonel, John Farquharson of Inverey, hid from the Redcoats. Photographing the Colonel's Bed, or even getting to it, was no mean feat with the amount of equipment they had to carry, and their task was made more difficult by their concern that they might run into the Laird. 'Dismounting about a mile up the glen,' wrote Walker, 'we sent back the dog-cart to the nearest farm – not being allowed to proceed farther for the chance of meeting his Lordship's vehicle on the narrow road, on which we must ride or be rode over, or toppled down the steep banks.' Not many years ago a great row broke out when the present laird widened the track to allow *his* vehicle to go up the glen.

This is how Wilson and his companion made their way to the Colonel's Bed.

Strapping our burdens upon us, we proceeded to climb the winding road and with some rests by the way soon reached a high elevation in the glen from which we surveyed a wild and dreary region where the streams tumbled down the faces of the hill making sheer leaps of hundreds of feet at a bound. The birch grew in thickets so close that they were almost impenetrable, the small stems being within a few inches of each other, while precipices yawned upon the water below us.

Descending by a footpath which numerous pilgrims had formed and for whom a series of steps were laid we reached the Colonel's Bed, a large long fissure in the rock under beetling precipices which appeared so closely above as almost to exclude the light of day, while deep and black pools lay hid in the darkness at our feet.

Trees clung to the rocks above and projecting their long tortuous roots along the face of the cliffs sent their branches down and across the chasm. Right opposite, a recess of the rock was filled from top to bottom with a waving mantle of ferns and wild flowers. Turning a sharp angle of the rocks, the valley opened up down the stream and some views were taken in the gloom in which the light, streaming round the edges of the rock, had a very peculiar effect.

11.3 *The Colonel's Bed, Glen Ey, Braemar (George Washington Wilson)*

Walker spoke about the excitement of taking pictures, likening it to the hunter stalking a stag or the fisherman gaffing a fish.

> Somewhat akin to the photographer is the moment when, with a plate in the camera and hand on the slide, he casts a hasty glance to the sky and then at the scene, removes the slide and then, with nervous anxiety, fearing to breathe lest the leaves rustle, counts the seconds, eagerly desiring that the little cloud may pass and allow the sun to stream out for a few seconds at the close, to gild the tips of the rocks, to burnish the rugged bark of the trees, to lighten the foreground with a living glory, and to stamp the picture as 'a joy for ever'.

The Falls of Garbh Allt (Garrawalt) in Ballochbuie Forest also came under Wilson's lens. Walker thought it one of the most attractive sights on Deeside. Queen Victoria's attitude to public access to the Falls was less rigid than it is today, although in recent years this has been changing. There was a fog-house (a summer house lined with moss) at the Falls in Victoria's time and visitors strolled across the 'handsome rustic bridge' spanning the river and picnicked in the fog-house. Wrote Walker:

> Several parties 'did' the Garrawalt that day ... The usual course of procedure was to drive up, walk round the bridge, look at the photographers instead of the view, enter the fog-house, and exit. From a spot about 250 yards east of the bridge and to which a footpath leads one of the finest prospects of Highland scenery is to be found which can anywhere be got – Invercauld House, the bridge, and the winding Dee being set in a framework of forest-clad mountains, while the bold cliffs of Bennabourd in the distance formed a noble background.

The following morning they 'bade a final adieu to Braemar' and as the coach rattled out of the village they asked themselves the question that had been in their minds at the start of their outing – had Braemar changed in the past twenty years. They recalled someone saying in 1833 that the people there had 'much honesty and great civility'. They never touched their hats when 'speaking to an individual with a good coat', and they never used the term 'your honour' or 'even the less respectful "sir"'.

'It will be interesting to mark the effect of cicumstances on such a community,' wrote Walker, 'and to inquire at the end of other twenty years if this is their character still. They may change, but nature around them will not.' With that philosophical thought, George Walker's report on their great expedition to 'the linns and corries of the Deeside Highlands' came to an end.

George Washington Wilson's Deeside trip set the seal on an ambition he had nursed since taking his first stereoscopic views in 1855. He wanted to supplement his income from portraiture by carving a niche for himself in commercial landscape photography. In 1856 he published a list of stereoscopic views which had forty-four views taken in sixteen locations in and around Aberdeen, including Braemar and Aberdeen. To sell his work he opened up a network of retail agencies throughout Scotland in stationery shops, bookshops and fancy-goods shops, as well as hotels, steamships and railway bookstalls. By the 1860s his photographs were on sale throughout Britain.

His fame as 'Photographer to the Queen' was also spreading; his first photographs of Victoria, Prince Albert and other members of the Royal Family were taken September 1855. The Queen also commissioned him to take landscape views, particularly views that she had seen and marvelled at on her Great Expeditions. It was John Brown who helped to open royal doors at Balmoral. He struck up a warm friendshsip with GWW and Walker noted that the Queen's personal servant 'kept his weather eye open and seeing how the wind blew made all things easy for his generous friend, Mr Wilson'.

There were other Victorian photographers who beat a path to the gates of Balmoral Castle in Victoria's time, but only forty-seven Royal Warrants were issued during her long reign; less than a dozen were in Scotland. Few of the holders ever saw inside the Queen's Scottish home, but one photographer who beat the Scots on their own ground – Royal Deeside – was a 'Geordie'. His name was William Downey, of the firm of W. and D. Downey, Newcastle, a carpenter from South Shields who had turned to photography. In the early 1860s he was the first to break Washington Wilson's dominance at Balmoral.

The picture that opened the gates of Balmoral for Downey showed a baby girl being carried pick-a-back by her mother – the sort of picture that most people would find in the family album. The mother was the Princess of Wales (later Queen Alexandra) and the baby girl being carried pick-a-back was her daughter Princess Louise. The picture was ahead of its time, showing an informality seldom seen in early royal pictures. Royal groups were normally placed against sober Victorian backgrounds, but Downey broke the mould. The picture sold 300,000 copies when it was made available to the general public.

Downey had already visited Deeside before Queen Victoria summoned him to Balmoral. In 1865, the year of the pick-a-back picture, he travelled north to Abergeldie Castle to photograph the Prince of Wales, who gave him many of his early commissions. Here again he showed how he could put his royal sitters at their ease. The bearded prince, wearing the kilt, was posed leaning casually over a chair, puffing his pipe, his walking stick between his knees.

Despite the competition, George Washington Wilson, Aberdeen's pioneer photographer, stayed ahead of them all. His biographer, Roger Taylor, said that this was because he knew how to go about selling himself. He was a 'damned good publicity agent', and a clever and skillful businessman as well as a good photographer. Wilson died in 1893, but his name is still known a century after his death – and his pictures are still selling. There are 45,000 of his glass negatives in the possession of Aberdeen University.

12

Forgotten photographer

An old sepia photograph of a Deeside shepherd called Charles Stewart lay in a drawer in my house for more years than I care to remember. He was my wife's great-grandfather. Born in 1826 at Pannanich, he herded sheep at Ballaterich, east of Ballater, tramping the moors where the poet Byron roamed as a boy. I found his picture buried in a bundle of old snapshots, gathering dust.

Only four inches long and two inches wide, the cardboard-mounted print showed Stewart sitting with his collie dog, wearing a plaid over his shoulder and holding a stick in one hand and a bible in the other. When I first saw it I was more interested in the man who had taken it than in the subject himself. I had been trying to trace the work of a Deeside photographer Robert Milne, who had photographed Queen Victoria in the last years of her reign, but who was virtually unknown. Now, by an odd quirk of fate, I had stumbled on one of his photographs: 'R. Milne, Aboyne,' it read. 'Portrait and Landscape Photographer.'

It was the start of a trail that was to lead me to Edinburgh, London, Windsor and back to Aberdeen, searching for Robert Milne's pictures – and his story. I was chasing the ghost of a man who had taken over the mantle of Aberdeen's pioneer photographer, George Washington Wilson, and whose royal photographs had found their way into national archives. There were more than 100 of his pictures in the Royal Archives at Windsor Castle and twenty more in the National Portrait Gallery in London. He took the last photograph of Queen Victoria before she died and then put away his camera for good. He became the forgotten photographer of Victorian photography.

Milne was born in Kenmare in southern Ireland in 1865. His family moved to Aboyne in 1872 and he set up in business in 1889. His house, Buena Vista, looked on to the Green from the main Ballater road and had a glass extension as a studio. People queued outside his studio to have their pictures taken on the day of the Aboyne Games and it was there that Charlie Stewart posed for his portrait. Milne took another picture of the shepherd many years later; Stewart had become a greybeard, he wore a bonnet on his head instead of a Glengarry and carried a coat over his arm. His old collie dog had gone, but

12.1 *Charles Stewart, photographed by Robert Milne*

there was another dog at his feet. By then, the Aboyne photographer had gone up in the world. He was claiming royal patronage before it was officially bestowed on him (he was appointed Photographer to Her Majesty in Ballater in 1896) and he was advertising his 'Royal Studios in Aboyne and Ballater'. He was a self-styled 'Photo Artist', a title he gave himself in a photograph showing a coach-and-four outside the old coaching inn at Inver.

He turned his back on photography when Victoria died. Nothing could be quite the same again. He felt that interest in photography would decline at the end of the Victorian era, so he moved to Aberdeen and set up a fish-curing business. In 1986 the trail I was following led me to the home of Milne's granddaughter, Mrs Margaret Mair, in Aberdeen. Inside her house I came upon a photographic treasure chest. Mrs Mair showed me two old albums packed with Robert Milne's pictures – pictures of Queen Victoria and other members of the Royal Family, landscapes, photographs of visiting circuses, cricket on the Green at Aboyne, curling at Ballater in 1901, all vividly mirroring life as it was on Deeside at the turn of the century.

The search for information about the photographs was slow and tedious. Although the royal archives at Windsor had a number of photographs by

12.2 *This was the photograph that earned Milne the title of 'Royal photographer'. Standing (left to right) are Princess Helena Victoria of Schleswig-Holstein; Prince Henry of Battenberg; Count Mensdorff; Beatrice, Princess of Battenberg; and the Duke of York (later George V). Seated: Princess Victoria Eugenie of Battenberg; Queen Victoria; the Duchess of York (later Queen Mary) holding Prince Edward (later Edward VIII); Prince Arthur of Connaught; and Prince Alexander of Battenberg.*

Milne it had 'no documentary records referring to him'. The Scottish Photography Archives, set up to research photography and to develop the national collection of photographs, could provide no information. The National Portrait Gallery in London sent an index of their Milne photographs, but indicated that it was not complete. It looked as if Robert Milne really was the forgotten photographer!

But, bit by bit, the pieces began to come together. The National Portrait Gallery index gave 1896 as the year in which Milne was 'active'. It was also the year in which William Downey, the Newcastle photographer, took the first cinematography pictures of Queen Victoria at Balmoral. Downey had been taking still photographs at Balmoral since the early 1860s, which put him in competition with Washington Wilson, but in the dying years of the century it was Robert Milne who was his main competitor.

In February, 1986, the *Press and Journal* ran a series I had written about the Milne collection. It aroused considerable interest, but it also created some confusion – because of John Brown's beard. Brown was seen in a picture attending the Queen's carriage, but it turned out to be Francis Clark, his successor. 'When one sees a bearded Highlander attending on Queen Victoria,' wrote a reader from London, Brown's is the first name which springs to mind.' There was almost a repeat performance in a similar picture which gave the name of the Highland servant as George Gordon. The same London reader wrote to say that 'he bears a strong resemblance to the famous John Brown'.

Just as I was wondering how I could sort out John Brown's beard from all the other hirsute Highlanders, I got a letter from Mabel Gordon. 'I was delighted on reading my "P&J" yesterday to find the photograph of my grandfather George Gordon (Geordie) at the head of the horse pulling Queen Victoria's carriage,' she wrote. 'It is a wonderful photograph.'

Mabel was formerly housekeeper to the Queen Mother at Birkhall. When I first knew her she had retired and for seven years had been living at the Blacksmith Cottages at the bottom of Knock Hill, just off the road to Birkhall. I remember her telling me that she always went to the top of the brae to see the Queen Mum arriving or leaving. The Queen Mother, who was often at the last minute and in danger of missing her plane, always stopped and spoke to her. On one occasion Mabel told the chaffeur and royal detective that she thought she wouldn't wait because it would make the Queen Mother late. They insisted that she took her place at the top of the brae, saying that Her Majesty would be very disappointed if she wasn't there.

Mabel recalled her father telling her that Queen Victoria had seen a bird and asked what it was. 'A whaup,' said Brown. Victoria asked what its 'proper' name was. Brown didn't know. 'I'll ask Gordon,' said the Queen. 'He'll know.' (A whaup is a curlew.)

Mabel had originally had a copy of Robert Milne's picture of her grand-father, Geordie Gordon, but had given it away to a cousin. Now she was anxious to get a new print to frame and hang on her wall. I was able to see that she got it and a few years later she was able to help me out by lending me another picture that hung on the wall of her home. This time it was a photograph of her father, Frank Gordon, who was head stalker at Balmoral. It showed him hauling in fishing nets on Loch Muick with King George V and the Duke of York, later King George VI. I had always thought that there were no fish in Loch Muick, for I had never seen anyone casting a line there, but I was wrong. Two boats were used on the loch by royal fishers in the years before the war, one carrying people up the loch, the other for angling. 'These fishing parties were good fun,' wrote Colin Gibson, the writer and artist. 'The trout were small. To augment the basket, the stalkers and some of their guests usually made a sweep or two with a net, keeping the best fish "for the pot", and returning the others.'

12.3 *Hauling in the nets on Loch Muick*

Oddly enough, I recently saw similar pictures in the possession of Winnie Smith, of the Leys, Tarland (see chapter 7), whose family served with the royal staff at Balmoral during Victoria's reign. The pictures showed a line-up of kilted men up to their knees in water as they hauled in a long line on Loch Muick. The picture appears to have been taken from the east bank of the loch, looking across the water towards Glass-alt Shiel.

Robert Milne, like all the other royal photographers of the time, took pictures of the family hunting and fishing, but he also turned his lens on a different kind of fishing. Guests at Balmoral often took part in tableaux vivants in which groups represented plays, paintings, scenes and sculptures. One of Milne's photographs showed a fishing tableaux performed by 'stalkers and ladies'. One lady-in-waiting wrote that the evenings at Balmoral were 'really quite cheery'.

Then there was the Big Top. There were marvellous things to be seen and heard when the circus came to Deeside in those halcyon days towards the end of the nineteenth century – a sacred elephant, thirteen lions and lionesses roaring simultaneously when members of the Royal Family came to see them, a bare-chested strong man, girl acrobats in tights and a top-hatted ringmaster. Queen Victoria *was* amused, for, like Robert Milne, she was an enthusiastic circus buff.

When Pinder's Circus set up their tents on Ballater Moor in June 1892, the Queen heard about the visit and arranged a royal performance by the River Dee. She invited local people to attend and watched the whole two hours' performance from her carriage. Milne's camera captured it all. Another Milne picture was taken inside the marquee when Mr Ginnett's Circus visited Deeside in June of the following year (the Queen is seen on a makeshift royal stand fronted by pots of flowers) and in June 1898 Sanger's Circus performed at Balmoral. 'Lord' George Sanger missed the first performance, but presented the Queen with a pair of Shetland ponies. He put on a special performance at Windsor the following year. Queen Victoria teased Sanger about his 'Lordship' title; the circus owner had, in fact, adopted it because 'Buffalo Bill' Cody had called himself the Honourable William Cody. 'I said, "Hang it! I can go one better than that. If he's the *Honourable* William Cody, then I'm *Lord* George Sanger."'

Milne took a photograph of one of Sanger's elephants, a white one, 'probably the only white elephant ever seen in the Western world'. When the Prince of Wales saw it he asked if it really was a sacred white elephant. Sanger replied:

Well, your Royal Highness, a showman is entitled to practice a little deception on the crowd, but I should never think of deceiving my future King. As you see, it is certainly a 'white' elephant – in fact, a very white

12.4 *Some of the performers from Sanger's Circus*

elephant – but only because we give him a coat of special whitewash
every day. The Prince thought it a splendid joke, more especially when
I told him that I was once offered the genuine article, but refused the
animal as useless for showing.

The circus performer who probably made the biggest impression on the
Ballater crowds was a fat man with a bicycle, Joseph ('Big Joe') Grimes, 'the
largest cyclist in the world'. He was 6ft 4in. in height and weighed in at 36
stone. 'Big Joe' would have gone down well with the Royal Family, for Queen
Victoria approved of cycling, although she wouldn't allow any of her family
to wear the new-fangled 'bloomers' that were all the rage with lady cyclists.
Milne took a photograph of Princess Victoria of Wales on her bicycle at
Balmoral, along with her pet poodle Sam.
   Cycling had become one of the great Victorian pastimes and another of
Milne's pictures showed a party of seven enthusiasts – four men and three
women – out in the Strathdon countryside. The women wore long skirts,

12.5 *Robert Milne's picture of his father, John Milne, Aboyne*

tight-waisted jackets with leg-of-mutton sleeves, bow ties and 'tammies'. The men wore spats, gaiters, knickerbockers and plus-fours. Milne's own family were biking addicts; his father, John Milne, who was road surveyor at Aboyne, rode an old penny-farthing bike. He is pictured by his son, magnificently bearded, on the bicycle. John Milne was also the owner of the first motor car on Deeside. It had originally been bought by Lord Granville, brother of the Marquess of Huntly, who was unable to start it. Milne was summoned to Aboyne Castle and told, 'If you can make this thing work, it's yours.' He soon had it on the road.

Although Milne used his camera to faithfully chronicle life on Deeside, his royal commissions were the real key to his success. The visit of the Shah of Persia to Balmoral was a milestone in his career. His photograph of the Shah

12.6 Unknown baby (though clearly a VIP, given the top-hatted retainer). This picture is thought to have been taken on an avenue to the castle.

12.7 *This arch was built in honour of Edward VII's first visit to Ballater as king. It was sited beside Robert Milne's studio.*

and his party at Glenmuick House, where he was a guest, was published in a number of illustrated papers. 'It brought my name into considerable prominence,' he wrote many years later, 'and a bit nearer my goal, an appointment as official photographer in Scotland to Her Majesty Queen Victoria.'

In the days when the great houses on Deeside were packed with house parties, the Queen often left the Prince of Wales to do the entertaining at Balmoral. When the Shah came to Deeside she had a special reason for putting the prince in charge of arrangements. She had been warned by the Princess Royal about what kind of man she was entertaining. 'The Shah of Persia', wrote the Princess, 'always has a lamb roasted in his room which he pulls to pieces with his fingers, distributing pieces to all his ministers and attendants, all sitting on the floor. He also throws his pocket handkerchief across the room at his Prime Minister when he has used it, upon which this dignitary makes a profound bow and puts the handkerchief in his pocket.'

Milne's photograph of the Shah at Glenmuick House showed him surrounded by grim-faced bodyguards with drooping mustaches and long coats. Curiously, the Shah himself was unaware that his uncouth habits had turned people against him. He was so won over by the Queen that he had her *Journal of Our Life in the Highlands* translated into Persian so that he could read it.

The crowned heads of Europe flocked in a steady stream to Balmoral and Robert Milne's camera was there to record their visits. Perhaps the most notable was that of Nicholas II, Tsar of Russia, with the Tsarina and their daughter, the ten-month-old Grand Duchess Olga Nicolaievna. Once again, the Prince of Wales played host, turning up at Leith docks with the Duke of Connaught to meet the Russian party when they disembarked from the imperial yacht. The Prince wore breeches, boots and the grey and red overcoat of the Kieff (27th) Imperial Dragoons, of which he had been made Honorary Colonel. The Tsar returned the compliment by wearing the uniform of the Scots Greys, of which *he* had been made Honorary Colonel. The Tsar wasn't wholly happy with the exchange of uniform: 'How unpleasant to have to say goodbye to our officers and crew in a foreign uniform,' he wrote to his mother, Dowager Empress Maria Feodorovna.

The journey to Ballater got off to a bad start; heavy rain fell and the train rocked so badly that the empress was almost sick, but once on Deeside everything went smoothly. It was a spectacular arrival, five imperial carriages with their escort of Scots Greys rattling up to Balmoral as dusk fell, bonfires blazing on every hill and the bells of Crathie church ringing out a welcome to them as they approached the entrance to the castle grounds. Inside the grounds the pipers were waiting. Unlike the Shah of Persia, who had 'thoroughly detested' the bagpipes, the Tsar of Russia loved them. He was overwhelmed by the welcome they gave him. While the pipes blew, kilted attendants were lined up holding blazing 'sownacks', heavy bog-fire torches used in Halloween fires. The Queen stood at the door of the castle while the pipers and torch-bearers formed a semi-circle as the first of the imperial carriages drove in.

> I was standing at the door [the Queen wrote in her journal]. Nicky got out first, whom I embraced, and then darling Alicky [the Tsar's wife, Princess Alicky of Hesse, the Queen's granddaughter] all in white, looking so well, whom I likewise embraced most tenderly. We all went into the Drawing-room. The dear baby [Grand Duchess Olga] was then brought in, a most beautiful child, and so big, after which Nicky and Alicky went to their rooms and I quickly dressed for dinner.

Sir Arthur Bigge, the Queen's private secretary, described the Tsar's visit as a 'Russian occupation'. His retinue was so big that a log-cabin village had to be constructed and Balmoral Castle was so full that the footmen's quarters were said to resemble the hold of a slave ship. Four laundry maids had to share a bed and space had also to be found for ninety four-legged visitors – Russian horses.

Despite the terrible weather, the guests were all packed off to kirk at Crathie on Sunday morning. 'The most awful stormy morning,' wrote Lady Lytton, 'but all was arranged for going to Kirk so we all went, for Her Majesty never gives in. It was very interesting seeing the two pews full of the Royalties and the Emperor and Empress standing by the Queen even in the Scotch Kirk, where all is simple and reverent.'

The Tsar complained that the castle was colder than Siberia and that his hosts insisted on taking him out shooting all day long. 'The weather is awful, rain and wind every day and on top of it no luck at all,' he said, adding dolefully, 'I haven't killed a stag yet.' This wasn't surprising, for when he was stalking he had an escort of an English detective inspector, an armed guard and a member of Russia's special service police. Relief came when the Prince of Wales left for Newmarket, where he had a horse running. 'After he left,' the Tsar reported, 'I had an easier time.'

The last commission Robert Milne carried out for Queen Victoria was photographing the memorial she had raised to her son, Prince Henry of Battenberg, who died while serving in West Africa. The memorial was placed deep in the Forest of Ballochbuie and Milne photographed it only a few days before the Queen left Balmoral for the last time. She had a feeling that she would not return to her Highland home. She died not long after at Osborne House. 'I lost probably the best friend I had ever known,' wrote Milne. The Ballater photographer's story ended with the Queen's death.

For me, however, there was another mystery to be solved – and another 'lost' treasure chest of Victorian photographs to be found. On some of the old Deeside pictures I had seen I found the initials 'WW'. I thought they were the work of the famous GWW, but I came upon a studio portrait which had the names of two photographers – Robert Milne and William Watson. The mysterious WW had obviously worked with Milne. Ironically, I found a clue under my nose at Ballater, for Watson was buried in the little kirkyard at the foot of Gairn.

My search for information about him took me to the home of Mrs Jean Young, in Kingsway West, Dundee. Her husband, who had died many years before, had been Watson's nephew and in her house was an album of his photographs. Here were royal pictures of Queen Victoria laying the foundation stone of Crathie Church, presenting Colours to the 2nd Battalion Queen's Own Cameron Highlanders at Balmoral, and watching the Braemar Gathering when it was held in the Balmoral grounds. There were also magnificent

12.8 *The scene at the laying of the foundation stone of Crathie church*

landscapes, photographs of castles and stately homes, and a scattering of pictures from the Montrose and Brechin areas.

Watson's wife came from Montrose and he himself was born at Laurencekirk. He joined the Royal Field Artillery as a young man, became valet to the colonel of the regiment, and later joined his service as a butler. He took his first photographs while working in England, but in the late 1870s moved north to Ballater and became a professional photographer. He got a number of commissions from the Queen and the royal household and claimed to work 'Under Royal Patronage', but he never held a royal warrant.

There was considerable duplication in the photographs taken by Watson and Washington Wilson, as well as in those by Milne, who came later, starting in 1889. Two pictures in the Watson album showed the Glass-allt Shiel at Loch Muick: one, with GWW on it, was a close-up of the building, while the second, carrying WW initials, showed the shiel from across the loch. It was almost as if the two men had been working together at Loch Muick.

The strangest piece of duplication came when the infamous Munshi was photographed standing at the side of the Queen in the Garden Cottage at Balmoral, with a dog at the Queen's feet. There were, in fact, two pictures, both taken in 1894, one by Milne in which the Queen wore a white shawl and had the black dog at her feet, the other by Watson in which she wore a black shawl and had a white dog at her feet.

There was an apocryphal story at one time about how James Valentine, the Dundee postcard king, searched Scotland for the holes made by George Washington Wilson's tripod because that was the only way he could get good photographs. That fanciful tale was not a million miles from the truth, for it was said that Wilson's competitors knew which pictures he had taken by keeping an eye on newsagents' and stationers' windows. They then chased around the countryside taking the same shots themselves; there was no such thing as a copyright view in those days.

The royal pictures of Robert Milne and William Watson, as well as their landscapes, often matched anything that the great GWW produced, yet more than a century later Wilson's pictures are still in vogue – and still selling – while those of Milne and Watson are forgotten. Why? To find the answer you have to go back a century to the day when fire raged through an old photographic studio at Ballater. It was in that little wooden building on the Braemar Road that Robert Milne carved out a niche for himself in the fiercely competitive age of Victorian photography. The business was taken over before the First World War by Joseph Bisset, who ran it as a family concern. Milne's negatives were stored there, as were those of William Watson, and all were lost when fire destroyed it in the 1920s.

13

The Munshi

The Garden Cottage, with its tall chimneys and tree-trunk pillars, dominates the lawn of Balmoral Castle. It is an impressive building, built of stone and wood from the forest of Ballochbuie. The rooms are furnished in Victorian fashion. Look into one of the windows and you will see candlesticks, a basin and ewer, a feather duster and a pair of Pickwick spectacles lying on a table. The beds are neatly made – and a chamber-pot stands ready at each bedside.

The first cottage on the lawn was a wooden building completed in 1863. It was occupied by the gardener and was known as the Gardener's Cottage, a name that stuck when a new building was erected. It was a much more modest affair, but Queen Victoria, who could see it from her window in the castle, fell in love with it. Two rooms in the cottage were set aside for the Queen's use, but later the gardener was moved into one of the granite buildings that were springing up all over the estate.

The two rooms in the Gardener's Cottage were Victoria's retreat, just as the two rooms at the Genechal were her retreat, or the rooms set aside for her by John Grant's wife at Rhebreck. The cottage was only 200 yards from the castle, yet it gave the Queen the privacy she always wanted. She used it as a Garden Pavilion, frequently working there on her despatch boxes, and she often took tea there, and sometimes breakfast. The doors were opened so that she was seated partly in the open air – if there was a nip in the Deeside air it never bothered her.

The year after the cottage was built the Queen had to temporarily abandon it, for the rooms were used as an isolation hospital for Lady Ely, Queen Victoria's lady-in-waiting, who developed scarlet fever. In 1873 and 1874 alterations were made to the building, but by 1894 the wooden cottage had fallen into disrepair and was demolished. A new stone cottage was completed in 1895. Victoria's grandchild, Alexander (Drino), Princess Beatrice's oldest son, and his tutor lived there for a time, as did other grandchildren. Today, the cottage is used by lady secretaries when the present queen is at Balmoral. During the summer it is seen by thousands of visitors.

In October 1897, shortly after the Queen's Diamond Jubilee, the Deeside photographer Robert Milne took a picture of the Queen in the cottage. The picture was published in the *Daily Graphic* and became known all over the country, fanning the flames of a controversy that grumbled on through the last years of her reign. It showed the Queen sitting at a table in the cottage working at her papers, with a dog at her feet. Standing by her side attending to some

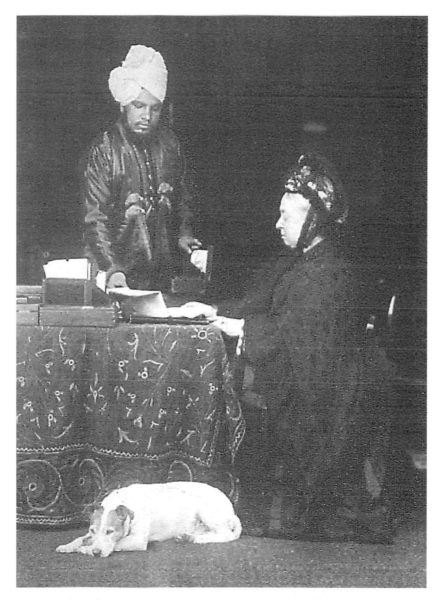

13.1 *This photograph by William Watson shows Queen Victoria in the Garden Cottage with her controversial Indian servant the Munshi*

13.2 *The Garden Cottage*

of the papers was the bearded, turbanned figure of one of her servants – the Munshi Hafiz Abdul Karim, Her Majesty's Indian Secretary.

The Queen employed a number of Indian servants. Sir Henry Ponsonby, her private secretary, once declared wearily, 'These Injuns are too much for me.' Abdul Karim was certainly too much for him, and too much for many other members of the royal staff. He was called an 'unctuous Oriental', and a 'low cunning sinister Oriental'. Malicious tongues called him the brown Brown, but no breath of scandal touched him in his relationship with the Queen, as it did with John Brown. The worst that was said of him was that he had far too great an influence over Victoria.

Munshimania seeped through the royal corridors like a contagious disease. It reached a critical point when the *Daily Graphic* published Robert Milne's photograph. By now, Karim had become fat and opulent looking. He is seen holding out a paper to the Queen. One report said he looked 'smug and super-cilious'. The caption read: 'The Queen's life in the Highlands, Her Majesty receiving a lesson in Hindustani from the Munshi Abdul Kairim CIE.'

The Queen, who did in fact receive Hindustani lessons from the Munshi, felt 'rather uncomfortable' when she saw the picture and its caption in the newspaper. She was 'terribly annoyed and upset' by the 'whole stupid business' and blamed the Aboyne photographer Robert Milne for sending the photograph to the *Daily Graphic*. It turned out that it was the Munshi himself who set the whole thing up. The Queen's resident doctor, James Reid (later Sir James), whose duties went far beyond looking after Victoria's health, got on his bike (he was a keen cyclist) and rode to Ballater to see Milne in his studio. He was told that the Munshi had ordered Milne to have the photograph of the Queen and himself published in the Jubilee number of the *Daily Graphic*. After Reid reported back to the Queen, he received a fourteen-page letter from her in which she exonerated Milne 'in this very annoying business'. But she added that Karim was 'so furious against you all that I do not advise any interview at present. I fear however Milne will say one thing to you and another to him. Better put an end to this story and don't try to bring about a possible scandal.'

Abdul Karim first went to Balmoral in 1887, the Queen's Golden Jubilee year. He was given a room that had been occupied by John Brown and in a letter to Dr Reid, Sir William Jenner, another royal physician, wrote: 'I am rather surprised that Abdul occupied John Brown's room. I don't believe in the ghosts of those long dead or I should expect one in that room.' Later, a cottage was built for him near the stables – Karim Cottage, which hides away in a clearing just off the main avenue to Balmoral Castle. It is a long, low wooden building with nothing to show that the Munshi and his family once lived there. Today, few people notice it on their way to the castle. In its original state, nobody saw it, for in the Munshi's time it was entirely surrounded by a twenty-foot palisade.

Mrs Bernard Mallet, one of the Queen's 'Extra Women of the Bedchamber', was sent behind the palisade by the Queen to visit the Munshi's wife. She found a fat lady in rich clothes and jewels living in a house that looked – and smelt – as if it had been plucked from the slums of Calcutta. It was said that Karim lived in terrible squalor. What Mrs Mallet, the Extra Woman of the Bedchamber, thought of the Munshi's bedchamber is not recorded, but members of the royal staff said that Karim's wife and mother-in-law were 'more degraded and dirty than the lowest labourers in England; spitting all over the carpets, performing "functions" in sitting room, etc.'

The palisade helped to keep the outside world from seeing what went on in this Indian 'settlement' only a stone's throw from Balmoral Castle. It is more than likely that Karim's Cottage had its *zenana*, part of the building reserved for women and girls in Muslim households. There was a good deal of gossip and speculation about what went on in the cottage. Dr Reid dropped a discreet hint. Describing what happened when he was summoned on different occasions to visit the Munshi's 'wife', he said that each time he called he noticed that 'a different tongue was put out'.

The endless stream of 'aunts' and 'nephews' descending on Balmoral also set tongues wagging. How much truth there was in the rumours is anybody's guess, but there is little doubt that Karim was promiscuous. In 1897 he contracted gonorrhoea, but when the Queen learned about it she decided to overlook it. The Munshi could do no wrong. There is little doubt that this sort of thing stoked the fires of racial prejudice. Many of the ladies and gentleman of the court took a jaundiced view of coloured people, but it was not an attitude shared by the Queen. She set Dr Reid the task of ensuring that her Indians were treated properly and shown proper respect. 'Pray take care', she wrote to him, 'that my good Indian people get one of the *Upper Servants places* and are not put far from our saloons, also so that they have every comfort so that they are warm at *night*. They must be near. I *hope* Francie [Francis Clark, her Highland attendant] has had no hand in the arrangements for he is very prejudiced and was not inclined to be kind.'

Not many members of the royal staff were inclined to be kind to Abdul and 'these Injuns'. They regarded them as intruders and resented Victoria's attempts to make them feel at home on Deeside. Reid, in a letter to Sir William Jenner, said that the Munshi was 'as much disliked by the Queen's family and the Household as John Brown had been, but whereas Brown's worst enemy could not have accused him of disloyalty the Munshi was highly suspect.'

Plucked out of obscurity, elevated from *khidmutgar* (male waiter) to Munshi (teacher), turbanned and dressed like an Indian nabob, he got too big for his royal boots. Dr Reid drew up a list of things about Karim that annoyed him, presumably arming himself against the time when the whole affair would reach crisis point. When the Queen travelled south by train, for instance, Karim refused to allow other Indians in any part of the same railway carriage as himself. He also banned the Queen's maids from using the bathroom and toilet and insisted on having them entirely reserved for himself.

When the Queen was in Italy, large crowds gathered around a shop window where there were ten cabinet photographs in a large frame. Nine of the photographs were of the Queen, the tenth was the Munshi – in the centre! The vice-consul was despatched to have the Munshi's picture removed, but the Italians still thought that he was *Principe Indiano* and that the photograph was there because the Queen was in love with him. Karim, however, thought that the newspapers took too little notice of him. He complained to the Queen, who arranged for someone to see that the newspapers mentioned the Munshi more frequently.

Just how much Victoria worried about 'her excellent Abdul' was seen when he was with the Queen at Windsor in February 1890. It was there that he got a carbuncle on his neck and Victoria wrote to Reid to say she was 'much troubled' about it. She was very anxious about them all, she said, but especially about her Indian secretary. 'Abdul is excellent,' she wrote, 'so superior in every sense of the word that I feel particularly troubled about anything being the matter with him.' The Queen visited the Munshi several times daily and 'stroked his hand'. Reid noted in his diary that she examined his neck and smoothed his pillows.

There were frequent complaints about the Munshi's bullying and his 'tyranny' towards the servants. Meantime, Reid had the impossible task of trying to humour the Queen while at the same time giving her a glimpse of the *real* Munshi. He also had to pacify an unhappy household. The Queen was often tactless in her dealings with the Munshi. In 1895 Lord Wolseley, who had been appointed commander in chief, was summoned to Balmoral. He was surprised to find an ordinary garden 'fly' waiting for him at Ballater Station instead of a royal carriage. A few days later, walking in the castle grounds, he stepped on to a pile of snow to let a landau pass. Inside it was the Munshi. In a letter to his wife, Lord Wolseley commented on the fact that an Indian servant had been provided with a carriage, 'while the Field-Marshal, at the head of the Queen's Army, drives in a Fly'. At the Braemar Gathering in 1890 the Duke of Connaught complained to Sir Henry Ponsonby that the Munshi was mingling with the gentry. Sir Henry told him that he was there by the Queen's order and if it was wrong it would be better for him to mention it to the Queen. The matter was dropped.

The bad feeling between members of the household and Karim worsened, reaching a crisis point when a message was sent to the staff from the Queen saying that they had to associate more with the Munshi. The rebellious members of the household agreed to stand together and resign if the Queen pressed the matter. It was a turning point in the whole affair, for Reid decided to go to the Queen and tell her '*all* I knew about the Munshi'. This time he drove his message home and the Queen admitted that she had 'played the fool about the Munshi'. She wept and begged to be 'let down easily'.

With this success behind him, Reid then turned his sights on the Munshi himself. He pulled no punches. He told Karim that his 'presumption and arrogance' had created a situation that could no longer exist. Everyone, including the Queen, was beginning to find out that he was an imposter. He was low class and *never* could be a gentleman. 'The Queen does not know *all* I have told you,' he wrote, 'because it would shock her greatly to know how completely you have deceived her and what a scoundrel you are.' Reid ended by warning the Munshi that if he ever tried to humbug the Queen again she would be told everything about him. 'Then', he concluded, 'her pity will be turned to anger when she finds out how you have deceived her and will only hasten your ruin.'

Victoria's eyes had been opened about her 'excellent Abdul', but when he occasionally slipped back into his bad old ways, she continued to defend him. She wanted everyone to stop talking about 'this painful subject', either amongst themselves or with outsiders, and she said they should 'not *combine* with the Household against the person'. The Munshi wanted her to make him a nawab, a title which implied regal dignity. When she said it couldn't be done, he tried to bully her into giving him the MVO (Member of the Royal Victorian Order) as a Jubilee honour, but the queen took advice and reluctantly turned it down.

Reid was bombarded with complaints about the Munshi and was expected by Victoria to turn a deaf ear to them. 'I would sincerely ask you *not* to give heed to all you hear', she wrote to Reid, 'and this extends especially to the shamefully persecuted Munshi. It is wicked to listen to idle stories which are distorted and exaggerated. You *must* not allow such stories to be told to you. It is injurious and ungenerous to a man who is totally different to us, and whose life is a very dreary one thanks to the treatment of those whom I will *not* mention but who must be suppressed. I *do* feel indignant.'

Reid, buffeted by the Munshi troubles, his health affected, went off to his home in Ellon to have a break from his royal duties, but a few days later received a letter from the Queen, who was 'worried and anxious' about the Munshi. When he returned to Balmoral the Garden Cottage affair had blown up. The Queen said that Reid should not have gone to see Robert Milne without telling her. 'The Munshi looks on you as his bitter enemy,' she said.

So it went on. 'That debbel' the Munshi, as one of his countrymen called him, still occasionally got himself into hot water, and the Queen still leapt to his defence, but by 1898 life in the household was calmer and more peaceful. The Queen had made it clear that there was to be 'no Gossip amongst the Gentlemen' and that the previous disturbances should be 'buried in oblivion'. Abdul Karim continued to live in Karim Cottage, but after the Queen's death he retired to Agra to live in another Karim Cottage, and died there in 1909. Sir Arthur Bigge wrote to Viscount Francis Knowles, King Edward's private secretary, saying: 'You will have seen that the Munshi is dead – I can have no regret!'

Michaela Reid, whose book *Ask Sir James* gives a fascinating insight into the relationship between Queen Victoria and Sir James Reid, believed that snobbery and racial prejudice were behind much of the repugnance felt about the Munshi. She accepted that Sir James himself was a snob, but she had little good to say about Abdul Karim – 'this odious Indian'. She said he was 'tactless, pushing and high-handed', insolent, a bully, an 'evil character'. There were no soft words of sympathy for the 'excellent Abdul'.

Who then spoke up for Abdul Karim? One man did. He was Robert Milne, the Aboyne photographer who took the Garden Cottage picture that was at the heart of the Munshi row. Thirty years after Abdul Karim's death, Milne, now living in Aberdeen, wrote a series of articles for the *People's Journal* about his years as official photographer to Queen Victoria. In the articles he wrote about 'my friend the Munshi' – and about his relationship with the Queen and members of the household. Milne thought that Karim was 'the most picturesque personage in the Royal Household'. He had no idea how this 'cultured Indian' came to be a member of the royal household, but he thought he had been brought to this country to assist in the Indian administration.

Milne regarded his appointment to the royal household as 'a magnificent gesture of friendliness' to India as a whole, but, he added, 'some of the small men in big jobs could not see the matter in that light'. Even in the quiet retreat at Balmoral Castle, he said, the Munshi could not escape jealousy. Trouble was continually arising through the Queen's alleged preferential treatment of her Indian secretary. 'Matters became pretty hot once after I had published a special photograph of Her Majesty receiving a lesson in Hindustani from the Munshi,' he wrote.

Sir James Reid told him that there had been a lot of talk and dissatisfaction at the castle over the publication of the picture. 'It may interest you to know', he said, 'that Her Majesty is considering the cancellation of your appointment'. Milne explained that it was the Munshi who had ordered him to do it. Next day, the Munshi arrived at his studio and asked him if he had had a visit from Sir James, then told him to write to the Queen telling her what had happened. The following day a messenger arrived from Balmoral Castle to assure him that everything was in order. 'The Queen says you are not to trouble yourself at all about the matter,' he was told, 'for someone has been telling fibs.'

Milne was asked on a number of occasions to photograph the Queen's household, and some members would ask him if the Munshi was included in the group. When Milne said 'yes', the reaction was 'I'm not coming'. They changed their minds when it was explained that it was the Queen's command.

'During my whole association with him,' wrote Milne, 'I found the Munshi a thorough gentleman, a man of strong, upright character, and most meticulous in carrying out his duty to his royal mistress.' Milne took many photographs of the Munshi in his private room at Balmoral and had many heart-to-heart talks with him. Karim, a strict Muslim, was 'deeply grieved' that professing Christian ladies and gentlemen at the court should act in so un-Christian a manner towards him. 'If it hadn't been his intense devotion to Her Majesty,' wrote Milne, 'I believe he would have gone back to his native India.' Milne said that the Munshi interfered with no one. 'Not once did I hear him make a disrespectful remark about any member of the Royal Household, but unfortunately I cannot say that of other members of the household in regard to the Munshi.'

That, then, was the Munshi. In the end he went back to India, but not all his fellow countrymen returned to their homes. For years I had heard stories about a graveyard on Balmoral where Indian servants who had died while serving Queen Victoria had been buried. No one knew where the graveyard was, or, if they did, they preferred to keep quiet about it. The only clue I had

13.3 *Tawgin, the Indian servant at Balmoral buried in the graveyard at Ballochbuie*

was a photograph of one of them with his name on the back of it – and a note saying he had been buried at Ballochbuie. But bit by bit the picture began to take shape. The final piece of the jigsaw slipped into place when I met Peter Gillan, whose father had been head gamekeeper at Balmoral. Peter was born at Karim Cottage and spent his early years there. He remembers it as a big house, and cold. He said that when the Munshi was there you couldn't see it at all because it was surrounded by a stockade.

Peter knew about the graves. He and his friends had played there when he was a youngster. The burial ground, which had been laid out beside a pool, *was* in Ballochbuie, on the slopes of a hill to the east of Balmoral Castle. There were no gravestones to mark the site, but I was told by Peter, 'Look out for the rhododendrons.' It was the rhododendrons that led me to the graveyard; the pool that Peter had mentioned was still there, but great masses of rhododendron bushes had closed in on it, hiding any trace of graves. It was almost as if nature had put a protective arm around the last resting place of those who were buried there, a world away from their own country. I came down off the hill and made for the castle, closing the final chapter on the story of the Munshi and 'those Injuns'.

14

The stuffers

When I walked through the stately corridors of Mar Lodge I felt as if I was being watched by dozens of eyes. They followed me down the carpeted corridors, into the dining room, through the drawing room and book-lined library, and up the magnificent stairway at the entrance hall. They were stags' eyes, and they were everywhere, blinking at me from an endless array of 'stuffed' deer heads that hung from almost every wall in the lodge.

There were big heads and little heads, red deer and roebuck, some carrying the names of the men who had shot them. They were the relics of a lost art – taxidermy, the art of the 'stuffer'. As I was guided through the building by the housekeeper, Mrs Sandra Dempster, I was thinking of all the famous people who had passed under these deer-hunting trophies, lairds and lords, dukes and duchesses, bankers and billionaires, princes and politicians, kings and queens. Mar Lodge has been host to many of Europe's royal families over the years. I was thinking, too, of the stags' heads that had hung from another Mar Lodge more than a century ago.

There have been three Mar Lodges. The first was a plain structure just behind the present building. In the middle of the nineteenth century the Earl of Fife built a new mansion at Corriemulzie, across the River Dee. At first it was called Corriemulzie Cottage, but this was changed to New Mar Lodge. Queen Victoria danced there at an open-air torchlight ball in September 1852, and in 1857 the ladies of the royal party returned from a ball at New Mar Lodge at five o'clock in the morning before going to the opening of the bridge over the Linn of Dee.

New Mar Lodge was once described as a 'shapeless old hunting lodge with verandas supported by rustic tree-trunks', but it had a unique appeal – a remarkable collection of stags' heads, some of them perched on the roof of the building. The laird was inordinately proud of them and in 1895, when the lodge was destroyed by fire, he ran frantically about crying 'Save the stags' heads! Save the stags' heads!' His call must have been answered, for many of them now decorate the present Mar Lodge and its ballroom.

The present lodge, completed in 1898, was virtually the creation of Louise, the Princess Royal, eldest daughter of Edward VII. She had married the Earl

14.1 *New Mar Lodge*

of Fife (he was created a duke as a wedding present) and drew the first rough sketch of the building. When Queen Victoria laid the foundation stone of the lodge a bed of cement concrete was prepared: on it was a stone weighing nearly a ton, with a cavity gouged out of it to take the items to be deposited there for posterity, among them coins of the realm and local newspapers. Whether or not there was something to tell future generations about the stags' heads is not recorded. Queen Victoria arrived in a carriage drawn by four beautiful greys and was taken to the foundation stone in a bathchair pushed by her Indian attendant Mustapha.

At a lunch before the ceremony Monsignor James Canon Paul, from Braemar, proposed the toast of the Duke of Fife. He said it was a happy occasion, but it was also a sorrowful one because it reminded them of 'the sad disaster that brought ruin upon the beautiful residence which the Duke of Fife had loved so well'. No one could have imagined that a century later history would repeat itself and that fire would once again rage through Mar Lodge. This time there were no cries of 'Save the stags' heads!' By a happy coincidence, the house was being rewired at the time the fire broke out and all the furniture, paintings, prints – and stags' heads – had been removed and put in store.

Today, the lodge has been rebuilt exactly as it was before the fire and everything is back in place. The only difference is that the lairds have moved out and the National Trust for Scotland has moved in, and now you can book one of five luxurious apartments – Derry, Macdui, Dalvorar, Braeriach or Bynack – and live as the lairds did. Provided you do it self-service – no cooks or butlers are supplied!

Sandra Dempster has been housekeeper at Mar Lodge for thirty-four years. She served under the Swiss brothers, Gerald and John Panchaud of Lausanne, who bought the estate in 1961 from Captain Alexander Ramsay. The Panchauds planned to open up a spectacular new ski resort. There was to be a ski tow behind the lodge, a huge car park, a restaurant, a cafeteria for snack meals, heated changing rooms, toilet blocks and a ski school. There were also to be lunches in Mar Lodge's historic ballroom.

Most important of all, there was to be snow-making machinery which would be used to cover an area of twenty acres. 'One thing they're sure of', wrote the *Press and Journal* in December 1963: 'there will be plenty of snow.' How wrong can you get! There were heavy falls of snow for the first few weeks, then – not a snowflake. Artificial snow was pumped over the hillside, but it turned to slush and hard ice. The result was that the project was eventually abandoned and the estate fell back on its original aim of catering for game and fishing sports.

Then came the American billionaire John Kluge, whose wife – a former dancer – was said to be attracted to the idea of being the Queen's neighbour.

14.2 *The present building*

It was Kluge who sold Mar Lodge to the National Trust (he and his wife are now divorced), but he retained two cottages on the estate and still comes back to Deeside.

When I walked through the building with Sandra Dempster, she had with her a bundle of old prints showing what various rooms had been like in the Victorian years. We compared the past with the present and found that little, if anything, had changed. It was this that created a feeling of reliving history. Each room, each corridor, opened a tiny window on the great days of Mar Lodge – the billiard room with the original billiard table still in use; the magnificent dining room with its marble fireplace and a bust of Queen Victoria on the mantelpiece; the boudoir (what secret intimacies did that hold?); the lounge and its grand piano; an impressive grandfather clock and chair from Abergeldie; and a picture of Princess Louise with her husband the Duke of Fife.

The duke and his wife were a comely couple, but I couldn't help thinking of what had been said about him: that he was coarse and selfish, had a fondness for alcohol, treated people with contempt, and used the language of a Billingsgate fishporter. Fife was eighteen years older than his bride; they were married in 1899 in the private chapel at Buckingham Palace. Queen Victoria, who had a soft spot for the duke despite his crudeness, or perhaps because of it, was delighted with the marriage. In a letter to the Empress Frederick she wrote: 'It is a very brilliant Marriage in a worldly point of view as he is immensely rich.' When he succeeded his father in 1879 his estates extended over 257,657 acres in Banffshire, Aberdeenshire, Morayshire and Forfarshire. Much later in their marriage the duchess became almost a recluse and spent her time fishing at Mar Lodge and the other estates.

In one of the rooms there was a photograph marked 'Aunt Maudie and Granny'; 'Granny' was Queen Victoria and Maudie was Princess Louise's sister and the youngest of the family. She was the Prince of Wales' favourite – and the best-looking of the family. A tomboy, she peppered her conversation with schoolboy slang. Mar Lodge would have suited her well, for she liked the outdoor life and loved dogs and horses. In 1895 she became engaged to Prince Charles of Denmark (later King Haakon VII of Norway) and married him the following year.

The hall in Mar Lodge, with its rich carpet, chandeliers and staircase, takes your breath away. Up on the landing, a document lying on top of an old kist sets out the family tree of the Dukes of Fife. On the walls the ubiquitous stags' heads look down on you; a tag on one reads, 'This deer was shot in Duff House Parks – 4 October 1797.' One of the Panchaud brothers also has his trophy – 'J. B. Panchaud' – whose 'kill' was on Beinn Bhrotain, a hill above Glen Dee.

We moved on to the bar. It is no longer a bar, but a meeting place for shooting guests before they go stalking. There is an odd assortment of heads on the walls, including, curiously, a buffalo head, but what dominates the room is an enormous stone-built fireplace. I had seen it before, but the years had slipped away since I last warmed my fingers at it. Now, seeing it again, I remembered how I had once come down from the hills to find that Mar Lodge was alive, if not with the sound of music, at least with the sound of voices. I remembered how walkers and climbers had huddled around the great open fireplace drinking beer and swapping tales about heady days on the high tops. It all came to an end with the new lairds. One day, perhaps, the National Trust will open up the bar again and bring back the sound of music to Dalmore, the Great Plain.

We left the lodge and made our way to the ballroom. Critics have described Mar Lodge as an 'overgrown chalet', dismissing its style as 'suburban Tudor', but, strangely enough, no one seems to have made verbal assaults on the ballroom. Odd from the outside, it is a good deal odder on the inside, its ceiling packed with deer skulls and stuffed heads. It is regarded by some almost as the eighth wonder of the world, by others as a grotesque spectacle. The ballroom was originally constructed at Corriemulzie in 1883, but when the present Mar Lodge was built in 1895 the ballroom was dismantled and moved to its present site in 1898. Some of the original builders wrote their names and dates on the beams, but these were all on the roof and not on public display.

There are said to be 2,500 skulls and stuffed heads on the ceiling; some even make it 3,000, but as far as I know no one has climbed up there to count them. This sort of decoration became popular in the late Victorian period; it was popular in southern Germany and Austria and is said to reflect the influence of Prince Albert on this area. Today, German hunters come to Mar Lodge to shoot and Willie Forbes, the local taxidermist, sends them home with their trophies, but whether or not there is still a place for the kind of mass display seen in the ballroom is debatable. The antlered heads in Mar Lodge have a certain nobility, but there is no Monarch of the Glen glory in the sight of empty skulls and eyeless sockets. The annual ghillies' ball and other social events were held in the ballroom in its heyday and a ghillies' ball still takes place there at the end of the season in October. The ballroom can also be rented for weddings.

When I left Mar Lodge I made my way to Mhile Dhorch, the dark mile, on the road to Inverey. I was looking for a cottage not far from the Gallows Tree, west of the Victoria Bridge on the road to Inverey. The cottage stood on a bank above the road, part of the rear of the building in a state of collapse. From it you looked down on a stretch of the River Dee known as the Stuffer's Pool, for the house at Mhile Dhorch, or Meildorrach, was once the workshop of

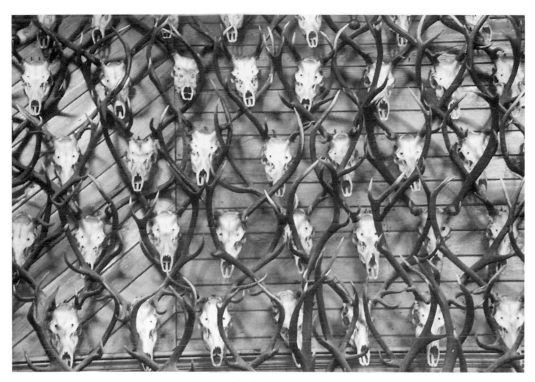

14.3 *The ballroom ceiling*

John Lamont, taxidermist to the Duke of Fife for fifty years: he was the man responsible for arranging the stags' heads and skulls in the ballroom at Mar Lodge. A testimonial to him said he was 'patronised by HRH the Prince of Wales and the leading nobility and gentry of Deeside and neighbourhood'. It was a glowing tribute to the man known locally as Jockie the Stuffer, and went on:

> John Lamont is adept in everything relating to the taxidermist art. He enjoys the exclusive patronage of his Grace the Duke of Fife, who has entrusted him with the preparation and mounting of many specially interesting and cherished trophies of the chase. The antler decoration in the Ballroom at Mar Lodge was devised and erected by Mr Lamont and the admirable result bears witness not only to his skill as a taxidermist but also to his powers of artistic treatment. The name of John Lamont is, in fact, one to conjure with among the sporting world of the Highlands.

In Victorian times most big estates had their 'stuffer', but to make a living they had to take other jobs. Jockie was also personal attendant to the Princess Royal and when his son Alistair followed his father into the taxidermy business he worked for the Duchess of Fife and Princess Arthur of Connaught, on one occasion accompanying the princess to England. Alistair, who helped his father to put up some of the Mar Lodge heads, also acted as ghillie to many of the wealthy guests who stayed there.

John Lamont was born in 1850. He showed his talent for taxidermy at an early age and King Edward VII took him to Bavaria to see a display of stags' heads in a ballroom there; he wanted the same thing to be done at Mar Lodge. Now, 2,000 'stuffed' heads hang on the ceiling of the Mar Lodge ballroom as a reminder of the days when taxidermy was all the rage. At one time, there were fears that when a ball was held the vibration caused by the dancers would bring the whole lot down and a net was hung underneath as a precaution. Today, they still seem immoveable, empty skulls defying any attempt to dislodge them.

An antlered head from Mar Lodge hangs in a house in Braemar. It was presented to Zan Grant, daughter of Alastair Lamont and John Lamont's granddaughter. Zan and Joe Grant hung it in the hall of their house, Myrtle Cottage, beside a small painting of the workshop at Meildorrach. The Stuffer's Pool is also shown in the picture. On the back of the mount is a faded piece of paper with the information that the stag was shot by Lord Macduff in 1898. Zan and Joe have given their stag a name – Jockie.

When he was due to retire, John Lamont built himself a house at Deeview, which lies to the west of Mieldorrach, looking across the Dee to Mar Lodge and the distant hills. He continued to do taxidermy work there after his retirement. Today, by a happy coincidence, Jockie's old house is occupied by the man who is carrying on the taxidermy tradition on Deeside. Willie Forbes, formerly head keeper on the Mar Lodge estate, has built up a considerable reputation as a taxidermist and a painter of skill and sensitivity. His first painting, 'The Drookit', showing a dead stag being brought off the hill on the back of a pony, hangs on a wall in Mar Lodge. Deer sketches by Landseer hang in a nearby corridor.

I went to see Willie at Deeview. On the wall beside the door was a framed copy of the testimonial to John Lamont. Inside Jockie the Stuffer's old workshop at Deeview I found Willie working on a roebuck which he had stuffed for an exhibition at Balmoral. Next door was a large landscape painting he had begun; it was to form a background to the figure of the roebuck. He was head keeper at Mar Lodge for fourteen years and still goes out with his old clients, some of whom invite him to their homes in Europe to shoot. Lately, he has been turning out a different kind of deer head, carving out small delicately-made *bronze* heads which have already proved popular with his clients.

I left Willie and made my way past Mieldorrach to Inverey, where there is a memorial to John Lamont. This, however, is not a memorial to Jockie the Stuffer, but to his ancestor, Johann von Lamont, a local loon who rose to become Astronomer Royal of Bavaria: his story is an extraordinary one. He came into the world as plain John Lamont, born at Corriemulzie, Braemar, on 13 December 1805. He was the only child of Robert Lamont, a forester to James, second Earl of Fife, who superintended the planting of great stretches of moorland with Scots pines and larches on the Upper Dee valley.

John got his early education at the school at Inverey and was one of its most brilliant pupils. He was said to be a bit of a star-gazer and it may have been the clear, bright nights on Upper Deeside that inspired him to study the heavens. In 1817, when he was twelve years old, a monk called Father Gall Robertson arrived in Inverey from Ratisbon in Bavaria. He was touring Scotland to find promising boys who could be given free education at a monastery in Bavaria – and in little Inverey he found Johnny Lamont. He was selected as a pupil, as were two other boys from Banffshire.

The story of the lad from Corriemulzie was first told by John MacPherson, a farmer at Woodhill, Braemar, in a memoir written in 1930 to commemorate the fiftieth anniversary of Lamont's death. MacPherson, a local historian, wrote the first guide-book on Braemar. In his memoir he described what happened when John Lamont left Braemar with Father Gall Robertson on his way to Bavaria.

> There were no stage coaches or other public conveyances running from Braemar in those early days. Even the mails were conveyed from the then nearest post town, Kincardine O'Neil, some 32 miles distant, by a walking postman who made the journey three times a week.
>
> Accordingly Johnny had to be conveyed to Aberdeen, the nearest seaport, by his brother-in-law, Donald Gruer, in one of his farm carts. Picture them setting out on a bracing October morning, the bottom of the cart well littered with straw, and the prospective student sitting on a wisp, his little trunk with all his belongings behind him, while Donald Gruer sat on the 'fore breasts' of the cart and guided the willing horse on his way.
>
> By mid-day they reached the wayside inn of Coil-a-Creich where they enjoyed a hearty dinner supplied by Mr Rose, the landlord (who was also the carrier twixt Upper Deeside and Aberdeen), and gave the horse a feed and a rest. Then they proceeded to Mr Ogg's at Heugh-head of Aboyne, another wayside inn, where they put up for the night.

Next day they reached Park Inn, near Culter, early in the evening, and as they did not wish to arrive in Aberdeen at too late an hour, they stayed there for the night. Early next forenoon they reached St Peter's Church, Aberdeen, where they were heartily welcomed by the Rev. Charles Gordon, the kindly, lovable and hard-working priest of the city and of many miles around. Here they also met Father Gall Robertson with two other boys, James MacNaughton and James Reid, from the Enzie district of Banffshire.

At the Scots Benedictine College at Ratisbon, John Lamont was trained for the ministry, but when the time approached for his ordination he decided it was not his vocation, and that he wanted to study astronomy. He left Ratisbon for secular studies at Munich University, where he became a professor of astronomy and built up an international reputation. Curiously, he had no ties with his homeland as he prospered in Bavaria. John MacPherson told in his memoir how, when a priest from Braemar visited him in Bavaria in 1842, he asked about his sister, Mrs Donald Gruer and her family, but appeared to have no link with his relatives in Braemar.

Johann von Lamont died at Bogenhausen, near Munich, on 6 August 1879. He never married. When a German newspaper reported that he had been born in Braemar, Queen Victoria, prompted by the Princess Royal (also the Crown Princess of Germany), made inquiries as to whether or not there were any relatives still living there. It turned out that John Gruer, a footman in the household of the Earl of Fife, was a grandson of von Lamont's sister Margaret, Mrs Donald Gruer, and that there were other grandchildren in Braemar, as well as a number of more distant relatives with the name Lamont.

In his memoir, John MacPherson traced these family connections. One section dealt with a Donald Lamont, who had married a Helen Farquharson and settled at Shenval in the upper part of Glengairn. Shenval, near Gairnshiel, is now a ruin. Donald and Helen Lamont had four sons, James, Robert, Andrew and Donald. Donald junior lived near Blairgowrie for some time, but eventually returned to Braemar and married Helen Thomson, Alanmore. They also had four sons – John, who became a taxidermist, Robert, Donald and James. This is what John MacPherson wrote in the final part of his memoir:

John was taxidermist to the late Duke of Fife, and personal attendant to The Princess Royal. He married Margaret Dow, teacher, Inverey, and had four sons, Alastair, John, Donald and Alfred, and two daughters, Margaret and Louise. Alastair married Edith Littlejohn, daughter of Mrs Littlejohn, Post Office, Braemar, and has a son and daughter.

Zan Grant, looking over my shoulder as I read John MacPherson's memoir, reached over and put her finger on the word *daughter*. 'That', she said, 'is me.' My search for a link between John Lamont, the lad from Corriemulzie who became Astronomer Royal of Bavaria, and John Lamont, taxidermist to the Duke of Fife, had come to an end.

After writing his memoir, John MacPherson planned to have 'a really worthy Lamont Memorial' built, but he died in 1931 before work could be done on it. The Deeside Field Club brought his efforts to a successful conclusion. The monument was designed by local historian Fenton Wyness and unveiled at Inverey by the Princess of Connaught in September 1934, fifty-five years after Lamont's death. The inscription on the north-facing side of the memorial reads: 'This stone commemorates Johann Lamont 1805–1879 who was born at Corriemulzie. His Name is written in the History of Science as Johann von Lamont, Astronomer Royal of Bavaria.'

There is no memorial in Inverey to John Lamont, the taxidermist. Apart from the ballroom display of skulls and head, the only other link with him is his workshop at Mieldorrach. There was a plan by the National Trust to take it down and rebuild it at Mar Lodge, where it would be fitted out as it was when John Lamont worked in it. Nothing so far has come of that proposal, but if the Trust intends to do something about it they will have to act soon before the workshop disintegrates. If the building is not too far gone, it would be a worthwhile venture. It would also be a fitting tribute to Jockie the Stuffer.

15

The kirk

Jamie Sim was a maker of besoms and scrubbing brushes, tramping the roads of Upper Deeside with them in the late nineteenth century. Besoms were brooms, and Jamie was known as 'Besom' Jamie. Popular with his customers, he was a familiar figure in the Crathie area. He could be spotted in a crowd by the clothes he wore; old moleskin trousers with legs that were too long and a clerical coat reaching almost to his knees. A dusty two-peaked cap covered his raven locks and an untrimmed beard ran riot on his face.

In September 1894, a royal bazaar was held at Balmoral to raise money for the building of a new church. It was an outstanding success, the attendance being boosted by special trains running from Aberdeen to Ballater. It lasted for two days and Queen Victoria visited it five times. 'Besom' Jamie Sim visited it only once – and was stopped at the entrance.

'Where are you going?' demanded a policeman.

'Tae the bazaar, o' course,' replied Jamie.

The 'bobby' eyed 'Besom' Jamie's clothes with an air of disapproval, then looked down at his unbrushed boots. 'You'll require to pay half a crown,' he said, thinking that that would end the matter.

'Wha dae ye tak' me for, man?' said Jamie angrily. 'It's plain ye dinna ken wha yer speakin' tae. The folk o' Crathie ken me better than they dae you. Mair than that, I hae plenty o' money, my man!'

With that, he marched up to the gatekeeper, slapped down his half crown, and marched into the enclosure.

What the policeman didn't know was that Jamie had donated some of his besoms and scrubbing brushes to the bazaar, and they were selling briskly on many of the stalls, alongside contributions from royalty. A report on the bazaar said that there was everything from a ship's anchor to a needle, ranging from a £50 chilled plough (made in America) to one of 'Besom' Jamie's brushes – 'an article of purely highland industry, viz., a *heather scrubber*'. It cost one penny.

The Balmoral stall sold a vast range of items made by members of the royal family: etchings on leather by Princess Maud of Wales, ornamental boxes brought from the Holy Land by Prince Henry of Battenberg, and a quilt by

166

15.1 *The Balmoral stall at the bazaar held to raise funds for the building of Crathie church*

Princess Beatrice. The Duchess of Connaught made embroidered cushions and the Empress Frederick gave a painting marked 'Sold £18. 18s.' This was high pricing, for most of the pictures on sale were marked from 3s. upwards. There were inkwells, bottles of perfume, Bohemian jam pots, aluminium trays, Japanese fire screens, handbags, pin cushions, children's clothing – and a stag's head.

The royal photographer Robert Milne (see chapter 12) turned up at the grand bazaar and found another photographer taking pictures – Prince Henry of Battenberg. He had turned photographer for the day, 'snapping' visitors and charging them 5s. for a 'Cabinet' photograph. Photographs of Queen Victoria and the royal family, taken by Robert Milne, were on sale. The Queen had her own list of 'buys', ranging from glass mugs to silver menu-stands and children's dresses. The grand bazaar ended with illuminations by 'Mr Brock of the Crystal Palace Company', who had arranged for 6,000 lamps and 1,000 Japanese lanterns to be hung about the field.

The takings for the two days was £2,400. Less than a year later, on 18 June 1895, the Queen was present at the opening and dedication of the new Crathie kirk. The building cost £6,000. No one could have thought then that a century later thousands of people would gather at Crathie on a Sunday morning to watch another Queen and her family drive past on their way to church. It was a custom that had actually started in Victoria's time, when people from Ballater and Braemar went to Crathie to see the Queen arriving at the kirk in a carriage drawn by a team of white horses. But Crathie became a tourist mecca long before the building of the new church; people were drawn to it, not by the Queen, but by John Brown. Six months after his death, coaches plying between Ballater and Braemar stopped regularly at Crathie so that passengers could alight and visit Brown's grave in the old kirkyard on the banks of the River Dee. According to Mrs Campbell, wife of the Crathie minister, Dr Campbell, as many as 100 visitors a day made the pilgrimage during August. 'You should charge a shilling a head,' suggested Lord Bridport. If they charged that today the funds of Crathie kirk would be in good shape.

There have been five Crathie churches, the first dating back to the ninth

15.2 *Crathie church*

century. The ruins of the second stand in the old kirkyard of Crathie, the third was built on the site of the present church in 1804. Queen Victoria and the royal family worshipped there. This kirk lasted for nearly a century, the last service taking place on 23 April 1893. The following day, demolition work began, for the new church was to occupy the same site. For a time, services were held in the old Iron Ballroom at Balmoral Castle until a temporary wooden church could be built. The 'timmer kirkie' was in use for two years and Queen Victoria took Communion there in the autumn of 1863.

Like the trippers of Victoria's time, people still come to the kirkyard near the river to see John Brown's grave, but they stay to wander around the ancient stones, picking out names they recognise, spotting the Queen's doctor, her housekeeper and her wardrobe maid; noting the gamekeepers and ghillies, the foresters and Highland attendants. Daniel Burgoyne, the Queen's assistant under-butler is there, and there are stones to the Thompsons, who ran the Post Office at Crathie for so many years. William Paterson, who was head gardener at Balmoral for forty-six years, is buried in the kirkyard, and John Spong, Victoria's 'travelling tapissier'.

The grave of Johanna Robertson, housekeeper to Queen Victoria at Glassalt Shiel, who died in 1900 at the age of forty-seven, is one of a number of burial places inside the ruined walls of the old church, almost as if the kirk had become desperate for space. There, too, is a memorial to the Symons, who ran the merchant's shop at Easter Balmoral. John Symon died in July 1876 at the age of sixty-two; his wife Christina outlived him by twenty-two years, dying in January 1898, aged eighty-four. Mrs Symon, who was held in high regard by Victoria, was declared 'hopelessly ill' before the Queen's Diamond Jubilee, but took on a new lease of life in time for the celebrations on Deeside. When she died two years later the Queen was at Osborne. She wrote in her journal: 'We had found her and her good amusing husband in the village when we first came to Balmoral in 1848 and we built them their new house and their shop. She was quite an institution; and everyone, high and low, used to go and see her.'

Three of the Symons' children died in childhood, James at the age of three and a half, Helena, aged two and a half, and Victoria, aged seven. Maria Isabella, Anne and Mary lived into their seventies. The daughters who took over the Merchant's, as it was called, were less popular. Princess Alice described them as 'inveterate robbers'. 'We used to foregather at the village shop kept by the two Misses Simons, who had been there since always,' she wrote. 'They were great friends and inveterate robbers who used to give us ginger wine to drink as a sop when they cheated us. All the house parties went there to buy the usual tourist things.' Today, the shoppie at the Easter Balmoral entrance to the grounds is still going strong, although not so many 'tourist things' are sold to passers-by.

The story of Balmoral is written in these faded old tombstones. Among them are the graves of Crathie ministers who were buried in their own kirkyard. One was the Rev. Archibald Anderson, who was present when the foundation stone of the new Balmoral Castle was laid in September 1853. He was minister at Crathie for twenty-six years and was remembered as the clergyman whose collie dog, Towser, always went to kirk with him. It followed him up the pulpit steps and lay there during the sermon, but if he went on too long it would rise, stretch itself and yawn. Mr Anderson left the dog at home when the Queen first came, but she told him she didn't want it banished from the kirk for her sake.

Victoria had a soft spot for another dog that wandered about the castle grounds. It probably felt it had every right to be there because it belonged to Sir Robert Gordon, the previous owner of Balmoral. For some reason or other he called it Monkey. Patricia Lindsay, daughter of Dr Andrew Robertson, the Queen's Commissioner at Balmoral, mentioned Monkey in her book *Recollections of a Royal Parish*.

> The grounds were at this time overrun with rabbits, and I shall never forget the exciting delights of hunting them with ferrets and Sir Robert's old dog, Monkey, one of the most sagacious of animals. As far as my knowledge of dogs goes, he was of a nondescript breed, more resembling an overgrown Skye terrier than anything else, but he had the brains which are sometimes the compensation of mongrels. He was a great favourite with the Queen, who speaks of him as 'Monk'.

Victoria mentioned him in her journal when writing about the cairn ceremony on Craig Gowan to mark the purchase of Balmoral. 'Poor dear old "Monk", Sir Robert Gordon's faithful old dog, was sitting there amongst us all,' she wrote.

Another cleric buried in the Crathie kirkyard was the Rev. Dr Archibald Campbell, from Lonmay. It was during his time that the decision was taken to build a new church, abandoning the old whitewashed church where Queen Victoria worshipped from 1848 to 1893. The Queen was fond of the auld kirk, but wasn't happy with the fact that in the open gallery she was under the gaze of everyone in the church. The Rev. Alexander MacFarlane, who was at Crathie for eighteen of his forty years in the ministry, is also buried there. He preceded Archibald Anderson. Both men were popular preachers. Anderson was said to have 'great kindliness of spirit', and the inscription on MacFarlane's tombstone said he was 'truly amiable'. The Rev. Charles McHardy was MacFarlane's successor, but if he had any kindliness of spirit or amiability it wasn't very evident when he was in the pulpit. It was said that he had a strong and forceful personality and was always ready to deal out damnation. He seems to have belonged more to the age when, as one writer put it, 'the lynx eyes of elders and deacons appointed to watch and pray were alert in every corner. Every rumour, every suspicion of ill-doing was reported to the Kirk Session.'

The old stones tell their tales, but some tell of more recent times. In the Farquharson enclosure is the grave of Frances Strickland Lovell Oldham, wife of Captain Alwyne Farquharson, the Laird of Invercauld. Born in Seattle, USA, Mrs Farquharson was a flamboyant, colourful personality who was often seen striding through Braemar with her long cape flaring behind her. She died in 1991 at Torloisk on the Isle of Mull, another Farquharson estate, and the words of a twelve-line verse on her tombstone are in sharp contrast to the sombre lettering on the ancient stones about her. The opening lines are as follows:

> Do not stand at my grave and weep,
> I am not there, I do not sleep,
> I am a thousand winds that blow,
> I am the diamond glint in snow.

Before I left the old cemetery I went looking for Jamie, not 'Besom' Jamie, but Wee Jamie Gow, another marvellous character from the past. Jamie was the beadle at Crathie; to put it in his own words, he 'howked the holes' (dug the graves) when a funeral was about to take place. Wee Jamie, as his name suggests, was a tiny man. He was bedevilled by the fear that if he dug the graves too deep he might fall in and never get out, so the holes he howked never reached their proper depth. In *Recollections of a Royal Parish*, Patricia Lindsay wrote about Jamie's grave-digging: 'The sanitary inspector was not abroad in those days and the occupants slept as soundly within three, as within six feet of the surface of the ground.'

Wee Jamie was the kirk bellringer as well as the beadle. Patricia Lindsay notes:

It was one of the sights of Crathie to me in my young days to see little Jamie Gow, very short and rotund, clad in blue homespun, with a broad bonnet on his head, pulling the rope beneath the belfry. The rope was short and apparently very great, and I fear I often watched in hope that the force of the pull would hoist Jamie in mid-air when the bell swung back. It always rung from the time the minister started to walk from the Manse up the riverside until he reached the church. There was no vestry, so on fine days he wore his gown, and many were Jamie's anxious looks for the approach of the black-robed figure.

Beadles, or 'beddles', belong to the past. There are only church officers now. As Patricia Lindsay said, country 'beddles' in old times were generally oddities, often in appearance as well as character, and Jamie Gow was no exception. He had his moment of fame, or almost his moment of fame, when the painter Carl Haag chose Gow – the 'little fellow like Sancho Panza' – as a model for his painting *Morning in the Highlands*. In the picture, Jamie was the man leading a provision pony up Lochnagar. John Grant, the head forester, roared with laughter at the idea of wee Jamie having a prominent place in such a painting. Sadly, however, another ghillie replaced him in the final painting. I never discovered Jamie's grave; perhaps he was buried elsewhere. Nevertheless, every time I walk into that old kirkyard I think of the little unassuming man, the beadle, who 'howked the holes' in Queen Victoria's time.

The bells still ring out at Crathie kirk, but not with Wee Jamie's rope. Another familiar ritual has also gone, for the voice of the old-time precentor has long since been stilled. An entry in the church's Minute Book in October 1888 announced that a Mr McFarlane had resigned as 'our Precentor' and that he 'was leaving the district at once'. On 20 December 1894, the kirk session 'took into their serious consideration the question of introducing music to the service of the church'. There were sufficient funds to buy an instrument – 'either a pipe organ or a harmonium'. The kirk session plumped for a pipe organ. It was said that Queen Victoria gifted a pipe organ to the present church shortly after it was opened in 1895, but there is no firm evidence of this.

At any rate, the kirk got its organ. By the end of the twentieth century it was showing signs of wear and tear. The congregation were faced with the possibility that it would have to be renovated, but the cost was mind-boggling – £200,000. It was decided not to renovate it, but to buy an Allen digital computer organ costing £15,000. The computer age had come to Crathie Kirk!

I went to the church to see Jack Martin, the custodian, who, I was told, could show me the new organ, but inside the kirk there was no sign of it. 'Where's the organ?' I asked. I looked around and asked again: 'Where *is* the organ?' Suddenly, a blast of music blew down from the other end of the church. Beside me, Jack was holding in his hand the kind of remote control you use to switch on a television set. This time, however, it was switching on a church organ. Jack handed me the control. I pointed it towards a tiny green light at the other end of the church, pressed a button, and a Handel concerto came floating down the aisles. I can now boast that I have played the organ in Crathie Kirk.

John Henderson, who has been session clerk since 1987, guided me through the pages of the Minute Book of the Kirk of Crathie, dating from 11

15.3 *Robert Milne took this famous last official photograph of Queen Victoria at Balmoral*

November 1886. One entry, dated 1896, was about a move to give the Free Church the use of a wooden hall belonging to Crathie Kirk. This hall was, in fact, the building used to house the congregation when the present church was being erected. During the last war it was used by the local school, then it became an outdoor centre for the RAF. Later, it was destroyed by fire, and it was on the site of the old 'timmer kirkie', not far from the North Deeside road, that John Robertson, the Glenmuick gamekeeper, built a house for his retirement (see chapter 5).

When I was looking through the Minute Book I found names I had come across in my wanderings in and around Balmoral: Belnacroft, Craigowan, Garmaddy, Clachanturn. There was a Margaret Gillespie from Clachanturn in the book and I wondered if she had any connection with the Jimmy Gillespie who built the gates at Balmoral. There was also a James Coutts at Clachanturn, the same James Coutts listed as a blacksmith in the 1891 Census. Another name that caught my eye was Annie Beddie, who was admitted to membership of the kirk in 1929. In October 1901 an entry recorded the gift of an umbrella stand by a Miss Symon.

So it went on, people, places and events leaping out of the past. On Sunday 28 May 1995, a service of thanksgiving was held to mark the kirk's centenary. A picture on the wall of John Henderson's house shows a group of dignitaries lined up to have their photograph taken with the Queen. The session clerk is standing next to her. Queen Elizabeth II took Communion at the service, just as Queen Victoria had done for the first time in November 1871. When Victoria continued to take Communion while staying at Balmoral there was a hullabaloo about it, and even the Archbishop of Canterbury and Gladstone were displeased. Queen Elizabeth had no such problems. She told John she had enjoyed the service and that it was only the second time she had taken Communion in the Church of Scotland, the first being at the General Assembly in 1976.

For the past four years the minister of Crathie Kirk has been the Rev. Robert Sloane – Bob Sloane to his parishioners. When they call him on the phone a voice answers, 'Bob here!' He is friendly and informal, popular with his congregation. From the outside, his manse seems enormous – a huge extension was added when the church was built in 1895 – but inside it is warm and comfortable. Bob showed me a room that had been part of the extension and was used to entertain Queen Victoria when she visited the minister. It was large and impressive, but Bob Sloane thought it a little imprac-tical in this day and age.

I couldn't help thinking of the sort of manse that would have been there in the early eighteenth century, when 'the whole value of the manse amounted to four hundred pounds Scots money'. It would have had a thatched roof, with a kailyard in front, and narrow little windows letting in dim light through walls three feet thick into low chambers and rooms divided by partitions.

The minister's lot improved as the years rolled by. Behind one wall of the

kirkyard, looking on to the River Dee, is a courtyard enclosed by farm buildings and a cottage. The stables for the minister's horses had once been there,
but now they lie deserted and unused. Bob Sloane and his congregation had
ambitious plans for the old courtyard. They raised a considerable sum of
money to build four self-catering cottages for people with disabilities, but an
application for a European grant was turned down. Two applications for
lottery grants were also rejected. The project was in limbo the last time I was
there, but Bob Sloane intended to try again.

The people who were to occupy these cottages would have had a tranquil
outlook, with the Dee almost on their doorsteps, Prince Albert's pyramid cairn
rising on Craig Luraghain, and golfers playing a round on the royal golf course
across the water. They might also have seen a mysterious 'table', with a large
circular stone top, standing on a prepared piece of ground on a path near the
old stables cottage, with a small sculpted figure on top of it. The sculpted figure
was made by a member of Bob Sloane's family.

The circular stone has a link with Crathie's vanished third kirk, demolished
to make way for the present church. It was once described as 'a severely plain
structure', and the Rev. Dr Campbell commented that 'a less pretentious
erection there could not have been'. Above the doorway of the church was the
circular stone that now lies in the manse grounds. The faded inscription on
the under side of it reads: 'This Church was built Anno Dom. 1804. The Rev.
Charles McHardy, minister.'